Profit

Over

People

OTHER BOOKS BY NOAM CHOMSKY:

American Power and the New Mandarins
Aspects of Theory and Syntax
At War with Asia
Cartesian Linguistics
Class Warfare
The Common Good
Critical Writings Vol. 1 and 2
The Culture of Terrorism
Deterring Democracy
Fateful Triangle: The U.S., Israel, and the Palestinians
For Reasons of State
Knowledge of Language, Its Nature, Origins and Use
Language and Mind
Language and Problems of Knowledge
Lectures on Government and Binding
Letters from Lexington: Reflections on Propaganda
Manufacturing Consent (with Edward S. Herman)
Media Control: The Spectacular Achievements of Propaganda
The Minimalist Program
Necessary Illusions
On Power and Ideology
Peace in the Middle East?
Pirates and Emperors
The Political Economy of Human Rights, Vol. I and II (with Edward S. Herman)
Powers and Prospects.
Radical Priorities
Reflections on Language
Rethinking Camelot: JFK, the Vietnam War and US Political Culture
Rules and Representations
Sound Pattern of English (with Morris Halle)
Towards a New Cold War
Turning the Tide
The Umbrella of U.S. Power
World Orders, Old and New
Year 501: The Conquest Continues

Noam Chomsky's publishers in the U.S. include Columbia University Press, Common Courage, Seven Stories, and South End Press; in the U.K., Pluto Press; in Australia, Allen & Unwin; and in Egypt, American University in Cairo Press.

Profit

Over
People

Neoliberalism and
Global Order

Noam Chomsky

SEVEN STORIES PRESS
New York • Toronto • London

In the U.K.:
Turnaround Publisher Services Ltd., Unit 3, Olympia Trading Estate,
Coburg Road, Wood Green, London N22 6TZ U.K.

In Canada:
Hushion House, 36 Northline Road, Toronto, Ontario M4B 3E2, Canada

Library of Congress Cataloging-in-Publication Data
Chomsky, Noam.
Profits over people: neoliberalism and global order / Noam Chomsky.
p. cm.
ISBN: 1-888363-89-4
ISBN 1-888363-82-7 (pbk.)
1. Free enterprise. 2. Liberalism. 3. Democracy.
4. Consumption (Economics) I. Title.
HB95.C516 1998
330.12'2—dc21
98-35985
CIP

9 8 7

Book design by Adam Simon

Seven Stories Press
140 Watts Street
New York, NY 10013
www.sevenstories.com

Printed in the U.S.A.

Neoliberalism is the defining political economic paradigm of our time—it refers to the policies and processes whereby a relative handful of private interests are permitted to control as much as possible of social life in order to maximize their personal profit. Associated initially with Reagan and Thatcher, for the past two decades neoliberalism has been the dominant global political economic trend adopted by political parties of the center and much of the traditional left as well as the right. These parties and the policies they enact represent the immediate interests of extremely wealthy investors and less than one thousand large corporations.

Aside from some academics and members of the business community, the term neoliberalism is largely unknown and unused by the public-at-large, especially in the United States. There, to the contrary, neoliberal initiatives are characterized as free market policies that encourage private enterprise and consumer choice, reward personal responsibility and entrepreneurial initiative, and undermine the dead hand of the incompetent, bureaucratic and parasitic government, that can never do good even if well intended, which it rarely is. A generation of corporate-financed public relations efforts has given these terms and ideas a near sacred aura. As a result, the claims they make rarely require defense, and are invoked to rationalize anything from lowering taxes on the wealthy and scrapping environmental regulations to dismantling public education and social welfare programs. Indeed, any activity that might interfere with corporate domination of society is automatically suspect because it would interfere with the workings of the free market, which is advanced as the only rational, fair, and democratic allocator of goods and services. At their most eloquent, proponents of neoliberalism sound as if they are doing poor people, the environment, and everybody else a tremendous service as they enact policies on behalf of the wealthy few.

The economic consequences of these policies have been the same just about everywhere, and exactly what one would expect: a massive increase in social and economic inequality, a marked increase in severe deprivation for the poorest nations and peoples of the world, a disastrous global environment, an unstable global economy and an unprecedented bonanza for the wealthy. Confronted with these facts, defenders of the neoliberal order claim that the spoils of the good life will invariably spread to the broad mass of the population—as long as the neoliberal policies that exacerbated these problems are not interfered with!

In the end, neoliberals cannot and do not offer an empirical defense for the world they are making. To the contrary, they offer—no, demand—a religious faith in the infallibility of the unregulated market, that draws upon nineteenth century theories that have little connection to the actual world. The ultimate trump card for the defenders of neoliberalism, however, is that there is no alternative. Communist societies, social democracies, and even modest social welfare states like the United States have all failed, the neoliberals proclaim, and their citizens have accepted neoliberalism as the only feasible course. It may well be imperfect, but it is the only economic system possible.

Earlier in the twentieth century some critics called fascism "capitalism with the gloves off," meaning that fascism was pure capitalism without democratic rights and organizations. In fact, we know that fascism is vastly more complex than that. Neoliberalism, on the other hand, is indeed "capitalism with the gloves off."

It represents an era in which business forces are stronger and more aggressive, and face less organized opposition than ever before. In this political climate they attempt to codify their political power on every possible front, and as a result, make it increasingly difficult to challenge business—and next to impossible—for nonmarket, noncommercial, and democratic forces to exist at all.

It is precisely in its oppression of nonmarket forces that we see how neoliberalism operates not only as an economic system, but as a political and cultural system as well. Here the differences with fascism, with its contempt for formal democracy and highly mobilized social movements based upon racism and nationalism, are striking. Neoliberalism works best when there is formal electoral democracy, but when the population is diverted from the information, access, and public forums necessary for meaningful participation in decision making. As neoliberal guru Milton Friedman put it in his *Capitalism and Freedom*, because profit-making is the essence of democracy, any government that pursues antimarket policies is being antidemocratic, no matter how much informed popular support they might enjoy. Therefore it is best to restrict governments to the job of protecting private property and enforcing contracts, and to limit political debate to minor issues. (The real matters of resource production and distribution and social organization should be determined by market forces.)

Equipped with this perverse understanding of democracy, neoliberals like Friedman had no qualms over the military overthrow of Chile's democratically elected Allende government in 1973, because Allende was interfering with business control of Chilean society. After fifteen years of often brutal and savage dictatorship—all in the name of the democratic free market—formal democracy was restored in 1989 with a constitution that made it vastly more difficult, if not impossible, for the citizenry to challenge the business-military domination of Chilean society. That is neoliberal democracy in a nutshell: trivial debate over minor issues by parties that basically pursue the same pro-business policies regardless of formal differences and campaign debate.

Democracy is permissible as long as the control of business is off-limits to popular deliberation or change; i.e. so long as it isn't democracy.

The neoliberal system therefore has an important and necessary byproduct—a depoliticized citizenry marked by apathy and cynicism. If electoral democracy affects little of social life, it is irrational to devote much attention to it; in the United States, the spawning ground of neoliberal democracy, voter turnout in the 1998 congressional elections arguably was a record low, with just over one-third of eligible voters going to the polls. Although occasionally generating concern from those established parties like the U.S. Democratic Party that tend to attract the votes of the dispossessed, low voter turnout tends to be accepted and encouraged by the powers-that-be as a very good thing since nonvoters are, not surprisingly, disproportionately found among the poor and working class. Policies that could quickly increase voter interest and participation rates are stymied before ever getting into the public arena. In the United States, for example, the two main business-dominated parties, with the support of the corporate community, have refused to reform laws that make it virtually impossible to create new political parties (that might appeal to non-business interests) and let them be effective. Although there is marked and frequently observed dissatisfaction with the Republicans and Democrats, electoral politics is one area where notions of competition and free choice have little meaning. In some respects the caliber of debate and choice in neoliberal elections tends to be closer to that of the one-party communist state than that of a genuine democracy.

But this barely indicates neoliberalism's pernicious implications for a civic-centered political culture. On the one hand, the social inequality generated by neoliberal policies undermines any effort to realize the legal equality necessary to make democracy credible. Large corporations have resources to influence media and overwhelm the political process, and do so accordingly. In U.S. electoral politics, for just one example, the richest one-quarter of one percent of Americans make 80 percent of all individual political contributions and corporations outspend labor by a margin of 10-1. Under neoliberalism this all makes sense, as elections then reflect market principles, with contributions being equated with investments. As a result, it reinforces the irrelevance of electoral politics to most people and assures the maintenance of unquestioned corporate rule.

On the other hand, to be effective, democracy requires that people feel a connection to their fellow citizens, and that this connection manifests itself though a variety of nonmarket organizations and institutions. A vibrant political culture needs community groups, libraries, public schools, neighborhood organizations, cooperatives, public meeting places, voluntary associations, and trade unions to provide ways for citizens to meet, communicate, and interact with their fellow citizens. Neoliberal democracy, with its notion of the market *über alles*, takes dead aim at this sector. Instead of citizens, it produces consumers. Instead of communities, it produces shopping malls. The net result is an atomized society of disengaged individuals who feel demoralized and socially powerless.

In sum, neoliberalism is the immediate and foremost enemy of genuine participatory democracy, not just in the United States but across the planet, and will be for the foreseeable future.

It is fitting that Noam Chomsky is the leading intellectual figure in the world today in the battle for democracy and against neoliberalism. In the 1960s, Chomsky was a prominent U.S. critic of the Vietnam war, and, more broadly, he became perhaps the most trenchant analyst of the ways U.S. foreign policy undermines democracy, quashes human rights, and promotes the interests of the wealthy few. In the 1970s, Chomsky, along with his co-author Edward S. Herman, began their research on how the U.S news media serve elite interests and undermine the capacity of the citizenry to actually rule their lives in a democratic fashion. Their 1988 book, *Manufacturing Consent*, remains the starting point for any serious inquiry into news media performance.

Throughout these years Chomsky, who could be characterized as an anarchist or, perhaps more accurately, a libertarian socialist, was a vocal, principled, and consistent democratic opponent and critic of Communist and Leninist political states and parties. He educated countless people, including myself, that democracy is a non-negotiable cornerstone of any post-capitalist society worth living in or fighting for. At the same time, he has demonstrated the absurdity of equating capitalism with democracy, or of thinking that capitalist societies, even under the best of circumstances, will ever open access to information or decision making beyond the most narrow and controlled possibilities. I doubt any author, aside from perhaps George Orwell, has approached Chomsky in systematically skewering the hypocrisy of rulers and ideologues in both Communist and capitalist societies as they claim that theirs is the only form of true democracy available to humanity.

In the 1990s, all of these strands of Chomsky's political work—from anti-imperialism and critical media analysis to writings on democracy and the labor movement—have come together, culminating in work like this book on democracy and the neoliberal threat. Chomsky has done much to reinvigorate an understanding of the social requirements for democracy, drawing upon the ancient Greeks as well as the leading thinkers of democratic revolutions in the seventeenth and eighteenth centuries. As he makes clear, it is impossible to be a proponent for participatory democracy and at the same time champion capitalism, or any other class-divided society. In assessing the real historical struggles for democracy, Chomsky also reveals how neoliberalism is hardly a new thing, but merely the current version of the battle for the wealthy few to circumscribe the political rights and civic powers of the many.

Chomsky may also be the leading critic of the mythology of the natural "free" market, that cheery hymn that is pounded into our heads about how the economy is competitive, rational, efficient, and fair. As Chomsky points out, markets are almost never competitive. Most of the economy is dominated by massive corporations with tremendous control over their markets and that therefore face precious little competition of the sort described in economics textbooks and politicians' speeches. Moreover, corporations themselves are effectively totalitarian organizations, operating along nondemocratic lines. That our economy is centered around such institutions severely compromises our ability to have a democratic society.

The mythology of the free market also submits that governments are inefficient institutions that should be limited so as not to hurt the magic of the natural "laissez-faire" market. In fact, as Chomsky emphasizes, governments are central to the modern capitalist system. They lavishly subsidize corporations and work to advance corporate interests on numerous fronts. The same corporations that exult in neoliberal ideology are in fact often hypocritical: they want and expect governments to funnel tax dollars to them, and to protect their markets for them from competition, but they want to assure that governments will not tax them or work supportively on behalf of non-business interests, especially on behalf of the poor and working class. Governments are bigger than ever, but under neoliberalism they have far less pretense to being concerned with addressing non-corporate interests.

And nowhere is the centrality of governments and policymaking more apparent than in the emergence of the global market economy. What is presented by pro-business ideologues as the natural expansion of free markets across borders is, in fact, quite the opposite. Globalization is the result of powerful governments, especially that of the United States, pushing trade deals and other accords down the throats of the world's people to make it easier for corporations and the wealthy to dominate the economies of nations around the world without having obligations to the peoples of those nations. Nowhere is the process more apparent than in the creation of the World Trade Organization in the early 1990s, and, now, in the secret deliberations on behalf of the Multilateral Agreement on Investment (MAI).

Indeed, it is the inability to have honest and candid discussions and debates about neoliberalism that is one of its most striking features. Chomsky's critique of the neoliberal order is effectively off-limits to mainstream analysis despite its empirical strength and because of its commitment to democratic values. Here, Chomsky's analysis of the doctrinal system in capitalist democracies is useful. The corporate news media, the PR industry, the academic ideologues, and the intellectual culture writ large play the central role of providing the "necessary illusions" to make this unpalatable situation appear rational, benevolent, and necessary if not necessarily desirable. As Chomsky hastens to point out, this is no formal conspiracy by powerful interests: it doesn't have to be. Through a variety of institutional mechanisms, signals are sent to intellectuals, pundits, and journalists pushing them to see the status quo as the best of all possible worlds, and away from challenging those who benefit from the status quo. Chomsky's work is a direct call for democratic activists to remake our media system so it can be opened up to anticorporate, antineoliberal perspectives and inquiry. It is also a challenge to all intellectuals, or at least those who express a commitment to democracy, to take a long, hard look in the mirror and to ask themselves in whose interests, and for what values, do they do their work.

Chomsky's description of the neoliberal/corporate hold over our economy, polity, journalism, and culture is so powerful and overwhelming that for some readers it can produce a sense of resignation. In our demoralized political times, a few may go a step further and conclude that we are enmeshed in this regressive system because, alas, humanity is simply incapable of creating a more humane, egalitarian, and democratic social order.

In fact, Chomsky's greatest contribution may well be his insistence upon the fundamental democratic inclinations of the world's peoples, and the revolutionary potential implicit in those impulses. The best evidence of this possibility is the extent to which corporate forces go to prevent there being genuine political democracy. The world's rulers understand implicitly that theirs is a system established to suit the needs of the few, not the many, and that the many cannot therefore ever be permitted to question and alter corporate rule. Even in the hobbled democracies that do exist, the corporate community works incessantly to see that important issues like the MAI are never publicly debated. And the business community spends a fortune bankrolling a PR apparatus to convince Americans that this is the best of all possible worlds. The time to worry about the possibility of social change for the better, by this logic, will be when the corporate community abandons PR and buying elections, permits a representative media, and is comfortable establishing a genuinely egalitarian participatory democracy because it no longer fears the power of the many. But there is no reason to think that day will ever come.

Neoliberalism's loudest message is that there is no alternative to the status quo, and that humanity has reached its highest level. Chomsky points out that there have been several other periods designated as the "end of history" in the past. In the 1920s and 1950s, for example, U.S. elites claimed that the system was working and that mass quiescence reflected widespread satisfaction with the status quo. Events shortly thereafter highlighted the silliness of those beliefs. I suspect that as soon as democratic forces record a few tangible victories the blood will return to their veins, and talk of there being no possible hope for change will go the same route as all previous elite fantasies about their glorious rule being enshrined for a millennium.

The notion that there can be no superior alternative to the status quo is more farfetched today than ever, in this era when there are mind-boggling technologies for bettering the human condition. It is true that it remains unclear how to establish a viable, free, and humane post-capitalist order, and the very notion has a utopian air about it. But every advance in history, from ending slavery and establishing democracy to ending formal colonialism, has had to conquer the notion at some point that it was impossible to do because it had never been done before. And as Chomsky hastens to point out, organized political activism is responsible for the degree of democracy we have today, for universal adult suffrage, for women's rights, for trade unions, for civil rights, for the freedoms we do enjoy. Even if the notion of a post-capitalist society seems unattainable, we do know that human political activity can make the world we live in vastly more humane. And as we get to that point, perhaps we will again be able to think in terms of building a political economy based on principles of cooperation, equality, self-government, and individual freedom.

Until then, the struggle for social change is not a hypothetical issue. The current neoliberal order has generated massive political and economic crises from east Asia to eastern Europe and Latin America. The quality of life in the developed nations of Europe, Japan, and North America is fragile and the societies are in considerable turmoil. Tremendous upheaval is in the cards for the coming years and decades. There is considerable doubt about the outcome of that upheaval, however, and little reason to think it will automatically lead to a democratic and humane resolution. That will be determined by how we, the people, organize, respond, and act. As Chomsky says, if you act like there is no possibility of change for the better, you guarantee that there will be no change for the better. The choice is ours, the choice is yours.

Robert W. McChesney
Madison, Wisconsin
October 1998

I

Neoliberalism

and

Global Order

I would like to discuss each of the topics mentioned in the title: neoliberalism and global order. The issues are of great human significance and not very well understood. To deal with them sensibly, we have to begin by separating doctrine from reality. We often discover a considerable gap.

The term "neoliberalism" suggests a system of principles that is both new and based on classical liberal ideas: Adam Smith is revered as the patron saint. The doctrinal system is also known as the "Washington consensus," which suggests something about global order. A closer look shows that the suggestion about global order is fairly accurate, but not the rest. The doctrines are not new, and the basic assumptions are far from those that have animated the liberal tradition since the Enlightenment.

The Washington Consensus

The neoliberal Washington consensus is an array of market oriented principles designed by the government of the United States and the international financial institutions that it largely dominates, and implemented by them in various ways—for the more vulnerable societies, often as stringent structural adjustment programs. The basic rules, in brief, are: liberalize trade and finance, let markets set price ("get prices right"), end inflation ("macroeconomic stability"), privatize. The government should "get out of the way"—hence the population too, insofar as the government is democratic, though the conclusion remains implicit. The decisions of those who impose the "consensus" naturally have a major impact on global order. Some analysts take a much stronger position. The international business press has referred to these institutions as the core of a "de facto world government" of a "new imperial age."

Whether accurate or not, this description serves to remind us that the governing institutions are not independent agents but reflect the distribution of power in the larger society. That has been a truism at least since Adam Smith, who pointed out that the "principal architects" of policy in England were "merchants and manufacturers," who used state power to serve their own interests, however "grievous" the effect on others, including the people of England. Smith's concern was "the wealth of nations," but he understood that the "national interest" is largely a delusion: within the "nation" there are sharply conflicting interests, and to understand policy and its effects we have to ask where power lies and how it is exercised, what later came to be called class analysis.

The "principal architects" of the neoliberal "Washington consensus" are the masters of the private economy, mainly huge corporations that control much of the international economy and have the means to dominate policy formation as well as the structuring of thought and opinion. The United States has a special role in the system for obvious reasons. To borrow the words of diplomatic historian Gerald Haines, who is also senior historian of the CIA, "Following World War II the United States assumed, out of self-interest, responsibility for the welfare of the world capitalist system." Haines is concerned with what he calls "the Americanization of Brazil," but only as a special case. And his words are accurate enough.

The United States had been the world's major economy long before World War II, and during the war it prospered while its rivals were severely weakened. The state-coordinated wartime economy was at last able to overcome the Great Depression. By the war's end, the United States had half of the world's wealth and a position of power without historical precedent. Naturally, the principal architects of policy intended to use this power to design a global system in their interests.

High-level documents describe the primary threat to these interests, particularly in Latin America, as "radical" and "nationalistic regimes" that are responsive to popular pressures for "immediate improvement in the low living standards of the masses" and development for domestic needs. These tendencies conflict with the demand for "a political and economic climate conducive to private investment," with adequate repatriation of profits and "protection of our raw materials"—ours, even if located somewhere else. For such reasons, the influential planner George Kennan advised that we should "cease to talk about vague and unreal objectives such as human rights, the raising of the living standards, and democratization" and must "deal in straight power concepts," not "hampered by idealistic slogans" about "altruism and world-benefaction"—though such slogans are fine, in fact obligatory, in public discourse.

I am quoting the secret record, available now in principle, though largely unknown to the general public or the intellectual community.

"Radical nationalism" is intolerable in itself, but it also poses a broader "threat to stability," another phrase with a special meaning. As Washington prepared to overthrow Guatemala's first democratic government in 1954, a State Department official warned that Guatemala had "become an increasing threat to the stability of Honduras and El Salvador. Its agrarian reform is a powerful propaganda weapon; its broad social program of aiding the workers and peasants in a victorious struggle against the upper classes and large foreign enterprises has a strong appeal to the populations of Central American neighbors where similar conditions prevail." "Stability" means security for "the upper classes and large foreign enterprises," whose welfare must be preserved.

Such threats to the "welfare of the world capitalist system" justify terror and subversion to restore "stability." One of the first tasks of the CIA was to take part in the large-scale effort to undermine democracy in Italy in 1948, when it was feared that elections might come out the wrong way; direct military intervention was planned if the subversion failed. These are described as efforts "to stabilize Italy." It is even possible to "destabilize" to achieve "stability." Thus the editor of the quasi-official journal *Foreign Affairs* explains that Washington had to "destabilize a freely elected Marxist government in Chile" because "we were determined to seek stability." With a proper education, one can overcome the apparent contradiction.

Nationalist regimes that threaten "stability" are sometimes called "rotten apples" that might "spoil the barrel," or "viruses" that might "infect" others. Italy in 1948 is one example. Twenty-five years later, Henry Kissinger described Chile as a "virus" that might send the wrong messages about possibilities for social change, infecting others as far as Italy, still not "stable" even after years of major CIA programs to subvert Italian democracy. Viruses have to be destroyed and others protected from infection: for both tasks, violence is often the most efficient means, leaving a gruesome trail of slaughter, terror, torture, and devastation.

In secret postwar planning, each part of the world was assigned its specific role. Thus the "major function" of Southeast Asia was to provide raw materials for the industrial powers. Africa was to be "exploited" by Europe for its own recovery. And so on, through the world.

In Latin America, Washington expected to be able to implement the Monroe Doctrine, but again in a special sense. President Wilson, famous for his idealism and high moral principles, agreed in secret that "in its advocacy of the Monroe Doctrine the United States considers its own interests." The interests of Latin Americans are merely "incidental," not our concern. He recognized that "this may seem based on selfishness alone," but held that the doctrine "had no higher or more generous motive." The United

States sought to displace its traditional rivals, England and France, and establish a regional alliance under its control that was to stand apart from the world system, in which such arrangements were not to be permitted.

The "functions" of Latin America were clarified at a hemispheric conference in February 1945, where Washington proposed an "Economic Charter of the Americas" that would eliminate economic nationalism "in all its forms." Washington planners understood that it would not be easy to impose this principle. State Department documents warned that Latin Americans prefer "policies designed to bring about a broader distribution of wealth and to raise the standard of living of the masses," and are "convinced that the first beneficiaries of the development of a country's resources should be the people of that country." These ideas are unacceptable: the "first beneficiaries" of a country's resources are U.S. investors, while Latin America fulfills its service function without unreasonable concerns about general welfare or "excessive industrial development" that might infringe on U.S. interests.

The position of the United States prevailed, though not without problems in the years that followed, addressed by means I need not review.

As Europe and Japan recovered from wartime devastation, world order shifted to a tripolar pattern. The United States has retained its dominant role, though new challenges are arising, including European and East Asian competition in South America. The most important changes took place twenty-five years ago, when the Nixon Administration dismantled the postwar global economic system, within which the United States was, in effect, the world's banker, a role it could no longer sustain. This unilateral act (to be sure, with the cooperation of other powers) led to a huge explosion of unregulated capital flows. Still more striking is the shift in the composition of the flow of capital. In 1971, 90 percent of international financial transactions were related to the real economy—trade or long-term investment—and 10 percent were speculative. By 1990 the percentages were reversed, and by 1995 about 95 percent of the vastly greater sums were speculative, with daily flows regularly exceeding the combined foreign exchange reserves of the seven biggest industrial powers, over $1 trillion a day, and very short-term: about 80 percent with round trips of a week or less.

Prominent economists warned over 20 years ago that the process would lead to a low-growth, low-wage economy, and suggested fairly simple measures that might prevent these consequences. But the principal architects of the Washington consensus preferred the predictable effects, including very high profits. These effects were augmented by the (short-term) sharp rise in oil prices and the telecommunications revolution, both related to the huge state sector of the U.S. economy, to which I will return.

The so-called "Communist" states were outside this global system. By the 1970s China was being reintegrated into it. The Soviet economy began to stagnate in the 1960s, and the whole rotten edifice collapsed twenty years later. The region is largely returning to its earlier status. Sectors that were part of the West are rejoining it, while most of the region is returning to its traditional service role, largely under the rule of former Communist bureaucrats and other local associates of foreign enterprises, along with criminal syndicates. The pattern is familiar in the third world, as are the outcomes. In Russia alone, a UNICEF inquiry in 1993 estimated that a half-million extra deaths a year result from the neoliberal "reforms," which it generally supports. Russia's social policy chief recently estimated that 25 percent of the population has fallen below subsistence levels, while the new rulers have gained enormous wealth, again the familiar pattern of Western dependencies.

Also familiar are the effects of the large-scale violence undertaken to ensure the "welfare of the world capitalist system." A recent Jesuit conference in San Salvador pointed out that over time, the "culture of terror domesticates the expectations of the majority." People may no longer even think about "alternatives different from those of the powerful," who describe the outcome as a grand victory for freedom and democracy.

These are some of the contours of the global order within which the Washington consensus has been forged.

The Novelty of Neoliberalism

Let us look more closely at the novelty of neoliberalism. A good place to start is a recent publication of the Royal Institute of International Affairs in London, with survey articles on major issues and policies. One is devoted to the economics of development. The author, Paul Krugman, is a prominent figure in the field. He makes five central points, which bear directly on our question.

First, knowledge about economic development is very limited. For the United States, for example, two-thirds of the rise in per capita income is unexplained. Similarly, the Asian success stories have followed paths that surely do not conform to what "current orthodoxy says are the key to growth," Krugman points out. He recommends "humility" in policy formation, and caution about "sweeping generalizations."

His second point is that conclusions with little basis are constantly put forth and provide the doctrinal support for policy: the Washington consensus is a case in point.

His third point is that the "conventional wisdom" is unstable, regularly shifting to something else, perhaps the opposite of the latest phase—though its proponents are again full of confidence as they impose the new orthodoxy.

His fourth point is that in retrospect, it is commonly agreed that the economic development policies did not "serve their expressed goal" and were based on "bad ideas."

Lastly, Krugman remarks, it is usually "argued that bad ideas flourish because they are in the interest of powerful groups. Without doubt that happens."

That it happens has been a commonplace at least since Adam Smith. And it happens with impressive consistency, even in the rich countries, though it is the third world that provides the cruelest record.

That is the heart of the matter. The "bad ideas" may not serve the "expressed goals," but they typically turn out to be very *good* ideas for their principal architects. There have been many experiments in economic development in the modern era, with regularities that are hard to ignore. One is that the designers tend to do quite well, though the subjects of the experiment often take a beating.

The first major experiment was carried out two hundred years ago, when the British rulers in India instituted the "Permanent Settlement," which was going to do wondrous things. The results were reviewed by an official commission forty years later, which concluded that "the settlement fashioned with great care and deliberation has unfortunately subjected the lower classes to most grievous oppression," leaving misery that "hardly finds a parallel in the history of commerce," as "the bones of the cotton-weavers are bleaching the plains of India."

But the experiment can hardly be written off as a failure. The British governor-general observed that "the 'Permanent Settlement,' though a failure in many other respects and in most important essentials, has this great advantage, at least, of having created a vast body of rich landed proprietors deeply interested in the continuance of the British Dominion and having complete command over the mass of the people." Another advantage was that British investors gained enormous wealth. India also financed 40 percent of Britain's trade deficit while providing a protected market for its manufacturing exports; contract laborers for British possessions, replacing earlier slave populations; and the opium that was the staple of Britain's exports to China. The opium trade was imposed on China by force, not the operations of the "free market," just as the sacred principles of the market were overlooked when opium was barred from England.

In brief, the first great experiment was a "bad idea" for the subjects, but not for the designers and local elites associated with them. This pattern continues until the present: placing profit over people. The consistency of the record is no less impressive than the rhetoric hailing the latest showcase for democracy and capitalism as an "economic miracle"—and what the rhetoric regularly conceals. Brazil, for example. In the highly praised history of the Americanization of Brazil that I mentioned, Gerald Haines writes that from 1945 the United States used Brazil as a "testing area for modern scientific methods of industrial development based solidly on capitalism." The experiment was carried out with "the best of intentions." Foreign investors benefited, but planners "sincerely believed" that the people of Brazil would benefit as well. I need not describe how they benefited as Brazil became "the Latin American darling of the international business community" under military rule, in the words of the business press, while the World Bank reported that two-thirds of the population did not have enough food for normal physical activity.

Writing in 1989, Haines describes "America's Brazilian policies" as "enormously successful," "a real American success story." 1989 was the "golden year" in the eyes of the business world, with profits tripling over 1988, while industrial wages, already among the lowest in the world, declined another 20 percent; the *UN Report on Human Development* ranked Brazil next to Albania. When the disaster began to hit the wealthy as well, the "modern scientific methods of development based solidly on capitalism" (Haines) suddenly became proofs of the evils of statism and socialism—another quick transition that takes place when needed.

To appreciate the achievement, one must remember that Brazil has long been recognized to be one of the richest countries of the world, with enormous advantages, including half a century of dominance and tutelage by the United States with benign intent, which once again just happens to serve the profit of the few while leaving the majority of people in misery.

The most recent example is Mexico. It was highly praised as a prize student of the rules of the Washington consensus and offered as a model for others—as wages collapsed, poverty increased almost as fast as the number of billionaires, foreign capital flowed in (mostly speculative, or for exploitation of cheap labor kept under control by the brutal "democracy"). Also familiar is the collapse of the house of cards in December 1994. Today half the population cannot obtain minimum food requirements, while the man who controls the corn market remains on the list of Mexico's billionaires, one category in which the country ranks high.

Changes in global order have also made it possible to apply a version of the Washington consensus at home. For most of the U.S. population, incomes have stagnated or declined for fifteen years along with working conditions and job security, continuing through economic recovery, an unprecedented phenomenon. Inequality has reached levels unknown for seventy years, far beyond other industrial countries. The United States has the highest level of child poverty of any industrial society, followed by the rest of the English-speaking world. So the record continues through the familiar list of third world maladies. Meanwhile the business press cannot find adjectives exuberant enough to describe the "dazzling" and "stupendous" profit growth, though admittedly the rich face problems too: a headline in *Business Week* announces "The Problem Now: What to Do with All That Cash," as "surging profits" are "overflowing the coffers of Corporate America," and dividends are booming.

Profits remain "spectacular" through the mid-1996 figures, with "remarkable" profit growth for the world's largest corporations, though there is "one area where global companies are not expanding much: payrolls," the leading business monthly adds quietly. That exception includes companies that "had a terrific year" with "booming profits" while they cut workforces, shifted to part-time workers with no benefits or security, and otherwise behaved exactly as one would expect with "capital's clear subjugation of labor for 15 years," to borrow another phrase from the business press.

How Countries Develop

The historical record offers further lessons. In the eighteenth century, the differences between the first and third worlds were far less sharp than they are today. Two obvious questions arise:

1. Which countries developed, and which not?
2. Can we identify some operative factors?

The answer to the first question is fairly clear. Outside of Western Europe, two major regions developed: the United States and Japan—that is, the two regions that escaped European colonization. Japan's colonies are another case; though Japan was a brutal colonial power, it did not rob its colonies but developed them, at about the same rate as Japan itself.

What about Eastern Europe? In the fifteenth century, Europe began to divide, the west developing and the east becoming its service area, the original third world. The divisions deepened into early in this century, when Russia extricated itself from the system. Despite Stalin's awesome atrocities and the terrible destruction of the wars, the Soviet system did undergo significant industrialization. It is the "second world," not part of the third world—or was, until 1989.

We know from the internal record that into the 1960s, Western leaders feared that Russia's economic growth would inspire "radical nationalism" elsewhere, and that others too might be stricken by the disease that infected Russia in 1917, when it became unwilling "to complement the industrial economies of the West," as a prestigious study group described the problem of Communism in 1955. The Western invasion of 1918 was therefore a defensive action to protect "the welfare of the world capitalist system," threatened by social changes within the service areas. And so it is described in respected scholarship.

The cold war logic recalls the case of Grenada or Guatemala, though the scale was so different that the conflict took on a life of its own. It is not surprising that with the victory of the more powerful antagonist, traditional patterns are being restored. It should also come as no surprise that the Pentagon budget remains at cold war levels and is now increasing, while Washington's international policies have barely changed, more facts that help us gain some insight into the realities of global order.

Returning to the question of which countries developed, at least one conclusion seems reasonably clear: development has been contingent on freedom from "experiments" based on the "bad ideas" that were very good ideas for the designers and their collaborators. That is no guarantee of success, but it does seem to have been a prerequisite for it.

Let's turn to the second question: How did Europe and those who escaped its control succeed in developing? Part of the answer again seems clear: by radically violating approved free market doctrine. That conclusion holds from England to the East Asian growth area today, surely including the United States, the leader in protectionism from its origins.

Standard economic history recognizes that state intervention has played a central role in economic growth. But its impact is underestimated because of too narrow a focus. To mention one major omission, the industrial revolution relied on cheap cotton, mainly from the United States. It was kept cheap and available not by market forces, but by elimination of the indigenous population and slavery. There were of course other cotton producers. Prominent among them was India. Its resources flowed to England, while its own advanced textile industry was destroyed by British protectionism and force. Another case is Egypt, which took steps toward development at the same time as the United States but was blocked by British force, on the quite explicit grounds that Britain would not tolerate independent development in that region. New England, in contrast, was able to follow the path of the mother country, barring cheaper British textiles by very high tariffs as Britain had done to India. Without such measures, half of the emerging textile industry of New England would have been destroyed, economic historians estimate, with large-scale effects on industrial growth generally.

A contemporary analog is the energy on which advanced industrial economies rely. The "golden age" of postwar development relied on cheap and abundant oil, kept that way largely by threat or use of force. So matters continue. A large part of the Pentagon budget is devoted to keeping Middle East oil prices within a range that the United States and its energy companies consider appropriate. I know of only one technical study of the topic: it concludes that Pentagon expenditures amount to a subsidy of 30 percent of the market price of oil, demonstrating that "the current view that fossil fuels are inexpensive is a complete fiction," the author concludes. Estimates of alleged efficiencies of trade, and conclusions about economic health and growth, are of limited validity if we ignore many such hidden costs.

A group of prominent Japanese economists recently published a multivolume review of Japan's programs of economic development since World War II. They point out that Japan rejected the neoliberal doctrines of their U.S. advisers, choosing instead a form of industrial policy that assigned a predominant role to the state. Market mechanisms were gradually introduced by the state bureaucracy and industrial-financial conglomerates as prospects for commercial success increased. The rejection of orthodox economic precepts was a condition for the "Japanese miracle," the economists conclude. The success is impressive. With virtually no resource base, Japan became the world's biggest manufacturing economy by the 1990s and the world's leading source of foreign investment, also accounting for half the world's net savings and financing U.S. deficits.

As for Japan's former colonies, the major scholarly study of the U.S. Aid mission in Taiwan found that U.S. advisers and Chinese planners disregarded the principles of "Anglo-American economics" and developed a "state-centered strategy," relying on "the active participation of the government in the economic activities of the island through deliberate plans and its supervision of their execution." Meanwhile U.S. officials were "advertising Taiwan as a private enterprise success story."

In South Korea the "entrepreneurial state" functions differently, but with no less of a guiding hand. Right now South Korea's entry into the Organization for Economic Cooperation and

Development (OECD), the rich men's club, is being delayed because of its unwillingness to rely on market-oriented policies, such as allowing takeovers by foreign companies and free movement of capital, much like its Japanese mentor, which did not permit capital export until its economy was well established.

In a recent issue of the World Bank *Research Observer* (August 1996), the chair of Clinton's Council of Economic Advisors, Joseph Stiglitz, draws "lessons from the East Asian Miracle," among them that "government took major responsibility for the promotion of economic growth," abandoning the "religion" that markets know best and intervening to enhance technology transfer, relative equality, education, and health, along with industrial planning and coordination. The *UN Human Development Report 1996* stresses the vital importance of government policies in "spreading skills and meeting basic social needs" as a "springboard for sustained economic growth." Neoliberal doctrines, whatever one thinks of them, undermine education and health, increase inequality, and reduce labor's share in income; that much is not seriously in doubt.

A year later, after Asian economies were struck a severe blow by financial crises and market failures, Stiglitz—now chief economist of the World Bank—reiterated his conclusions (Keynote Address, updated, *Annual World Bank Conference on Development Economics 1997*, World Bank 1998, Wider Annual Lectures 2, 1998). "The current crisis in East Asia is not a refutation of the East Asian miracle," he wrote. "The basic facts remain: no other region in the world has ever had income rise so dramatically and seen so many people move out of poverty in such a short time." The "amazing achievements" are highlighted by the tenfold growth of per capita income in South Korea in three decades, an unprecedented success, with "heavy doses of government involvement" in violation of the Washington consensus, but in accord with economic development in the U.S. and Europe, he correctly adds. "Far from a refutation of the East Asian miracle," he concluded, the "serious financial turmoil" in Asia "may, in part, be the result of departing from the strategies that have served these countries so well, including well-regulated financial markets"—an abandonment of successful strategies in response to Western pressures, in no small measure. Other specialists have expressed similar views, often more forcefully.

The comparison of East Asia and Latin America is striking. Latin America has the world's worst record for inequality, East Asia among the best. The same holds for education, health, and social welfare generally. Imports to Latin America are heavily skewed toward consumption for the rich; in East Asia, toward productive investment. Capital flight from Latin America has approached the scale of the crushing debt; in East Asia it had been tightly controlled until very recently. In Latin America, the wealthy are generally exempt from social obligations, including taxes. The problem of Latin America is not "populism," Brazilian economist Bresser Pereira points out, but "subjection of the state to the rich." East Asia differs sharply.

Latin American economies have also been more open to foreign investment. Since the 1950s, foreign multinationals have "controlled far larger shares of industrial production" in Latin America than in the East Asian success stories, the UN analysts of trade and development (UNCTAD) report. Even the World Bank concedes that the foreign investment and privatization it hails "has tended to substitute for other capital flows" in Latin America, transferring control and sending profits abroad. The bank also recognizes that prices in Japan, Korea, and Taiwan deviated more from market prices than those of India, Brazil, Mexico, Venezuela, and other alleged interventionists, while the most interventionist and price-distorting government of all, China, is the Bank's favorite and fastest growing borrower. And studies of the World Bank on the lessons of Chile have avoided the fact that nationalized copper firms are a major source of Chile's export revenues, to mention only one of many examples.

It seems that openness to the international economy has carried a significant cost for Latin America, along with its failure to control capital and the rich, not just labor and the poor. Of course, sectors of the population benefit, as in the colonial era. The fact that they are as dedicated to the doctrines of the "religion" as foreign investors should come as no surprise.

The role of state management and initiative in the successful economies should be a familiar story. A related question is how the third world became what it is today. The issue is discussed by the eminent economic historian Paul Bairoch. In an important recent study he points out that "there is no doubt that the third world's compulsory economic liberalism in the nineteenth century is a major element in explaining the delay in its industrialization" and in the very revealing case of India, the "process of de-industrialization" that converted the industrial workshop and trading center of the world to a deeply impoverished agricultural society, suffering a sharp decline in real wages, food consumption, and availability of other simple commodities. "India was only the first major casualty in a very long list," Bairoch observes, including "even politically independent third world countries [that] were forced to open their markets to Western products." Meanwhile Western societies protected themselves from market discipline, and developed.

Varieties of Neoliberal Doctrine

That brings us to another important feature of modern history. Free market doctrine comes in two varieties. The first is the official doctrine imposed on the defenseless. The second is what we might call "really existing free market doctrine": market discipline is good for you, but not for me, except for temporary advantage. It is "really existing doctrine" that has reigned since the seventeenth century, when Britain emerged as Europe's most advanced developmental state, with radical increases in taxation and efficient public administration to organize the fiscal and military activities of the state, which became "the largest single actor in the economy" and its global expansion, according to British historian John Brewer.

Britain did finally turn to liberal internationalism—in 1846, after 150 years of protectionism, violence, and state power had placed it far ahead of any competitor. But the turn to the market had significant reservations. Forty percent of British textiles continued to go to colonized India, and much the same was true of British exports generally. British steel was kept from U.S. markets by very high tariffs that enabled the United States to develop its own steel industry. But India and other colonies were still available, and remained so when British steel was priced out of international markets. India is an instructive case; it produced as much iron as all of Europe in the late eighteenth century, and British engineers were studying more advanced Indian steel manufacturing techniques in 1820 to try to close "the technological gap." Bombay was producing locomotives at competitive levels when the railway boom began. But really existing free market doctrine destroyed these sectors of Indian industry just as it had destroyed textiles, shipbuilding, and other industries that were advanced by the standards of the day. The United States and Japan, in contrast, had escaped European control, and could adopt Britain's model of market interference.

When Japanese competition proved to be too much to handle, England simply called off the game: the empire was effectively closed to Japanese exports, part of the background of World War II. Indian manufacturers asked for protection at the same time—but against England, not Japan. No such luck, under really existing free market doctrine.

With the abandonment of its restricted version of laissez-faire in the 1930s, the British government turned to more direct intervention into the domestic economy as well. Within a few years machine tool output increased five times, along with a boom in chemicals, steel, aerospace, and a host of new industries, "an unsung new wave of industrial revolution," economic analyst Will Hutton writes. State-controlled industry enabled Britain to outproduce Germany during the war, even to narrow the gap with the U.S., which was then undergoing its own dramatic economic expansion as corporate managers took over the state-coordinated wartime economy.

A century after England turned to a form of liberal internationalism, the United States followed the same course. After 150 years of protectionism and violence, the United States had become by far the richest and most powerful country in the world and, like England before it, came to perceive the merits of a "level playing field," on which it could expect to crush any competitor. But like England, the United States had crucial reservations.

One was that Washington used its power to bar independent development elsewhere, as England had done. In Latin America, Egypt, South Asia, and elsewhere, development was to be "complementary," not "competitive." There was also large-scale interference with trade. For example, Marshall Plan aid was tied to purchase of U.S. agricultural products, part of the reason why the U.S. share in world trade in grains increased from less than 10 percent before the war to more than half by 1950, while Argentine exports reduced by two-thirds. U.S. Food for Peace aid was also used both to subsidize U.S. agribusiness and shipping and to undercut foreign producers, among other measures to prevent independent development. The virtual destruction of Colombia's wheat growing by such means is one of the factors in the growth of the drug industry, which has been further accelerated throughout the Andean region by the neoliberal policies of the past few years. Kenya's textile industry collapsed in 1994 when the Clinton Administration imposed a quota, barring the path to development that has been followed by every industrial country, while "African reformers" are warned that they must make more progress in improving the conditions for business operations and "sealing in free-market reforms" with trade and investment policies that meet the requirements of Western investors.

These are only scattered illustrations.

The most important departures from free market doctrine, however, lie elsewhere. One fundamental component of free trade theory is that public subsidies are not allowed. But after World War II, U.S. business leaders expected that the economy would head right back to depression without state intervention. They also insisted that advanced industry—specifically aircraft, though the conclusion was more general—"cannot satisfactorily exist in a pure, competitive, unsubsidized, 'free enterprise' economy" and that "the government is their only possible savior." I am quoting the major business press, which also recognized that the Pentagon system would be the best way to transfer costs to the public. They understood that social spending could play the same stimulative role, but it is not a direct subsidy to the corporate sector, it has democratizing effects, and it is redistributive. Military spending has none of these defects.

It is also easy to sell. President Truman's Air Force Secretary put the matter simply: we should not use the word "subsidy," he said; the word we should use is "security." He made sure that the military budget would "meet the requirements of the aircraft industry," as he put it. One consequence is that civilian aircraft is now the country's leading export, and the huge travel and tourism industry, aircraft-based, is the source of major profits.

Thus it was quite appropriate for Clinton to choose Boeing as "a model for companies across America" as he preached his "new vision" of the free market future at the Asia-Pacific Summit in 1993, to much acclaim. A fine example of really existing markets, civilian aircraft production is now mostly in the hands of two firms, Boeing-McDonald and Airbus, each of which owes its existence and success to large-scale public subsidy. The same pattern prevails in computers and electronics generally, automation, biotechnology, communications, in fact just about every dynamic sector of the economy.

There was no need to explain the doctrines of "really existing free market capitalism" to the Reagan Administration. They were masters of the art, extolling the glories of the market to the poor while boasting proudly to the business world that Reagan had "granted more import relief to U.S. industry than any of his predecessors in more than half a century"—which is far too modest; they surpassed all predecessors combined, as they "presided over the greatest swing toward protectionism since the 1930s," *Foreign Affairs* commented in a review of the decade. Without these and other extreme measures of market interference, it is doubtful that the steel, automotive, machine tool, or semiconductor industries would have survived Japanese competition, or been able to forge ahead in emerging technologies, with broad effects through the economy. That experience illustrates once again that "the conventional wisdom" is "full of holes," another review of the Reagan record in *Foreign Affairs* points out. But the conventional wisdom retains its virtues as an ideological weapon to discipline the defenseless.

The United States and Japan have both just announced major new programs for government funding of advanced technology (aircraft and semiconductors, respectively) to sustain the private industrial sector by public subsidy.

To illustrate "really existing free market theory" with a different measure, an extensive study of transnational corporations (TNCs) by Winfried Ruigrock and Rob van Tulder found that "virtually all of the world's largest core firms have experienced a decisive influence from government policies and/or trade barriers on their strategy and competitive position," and "at least twenty companies in the 1993 Fortune 100 would not have survived at all as independent companies, if they had not been saved by their respective governments," by socializing losses or by simple state takeover when they were in trouble. One is the leading employer in Gingrich's deeply conservative district, Lockheed, saved from collapse by huge government loan guarantees. The same study points out that government intervention, which has "been the rule rather than the exception over the past two centuries... has played a key role in the development and diffusion of many product and process innovations—particularly in aerospace, electronics, modern agriculture, materials technologies, energy, and transportation technology," as well as telecommunications and information technologies generally (the Internet and World Wide Web are striking recent examples), and in earlier days, textiles and steel, and of course, energy. Government policies "have been an overwhelming force in shaping the strategies and competitiveness of the world's largest firms." Other technical studies confirm these conclusions.

There is much more to say about these matters, but one conclusion seems fairly clear: the approved doctrines are crafted and employed for reasons of power and profit. Contemporary "experiments" follow a familiar pattern when they take the form of "socialism for the rich" within a system of global corporate mercantilism in which "trade" consists in substantial measure of centrally managed transactions within single firms, huge institutions linked to their competitors by strategic alliances, all of them tyrannical in internal structure, designed to undermine democratic decision making and to safeguard the masters from market discipline. It is the poor and defenseless who are to be instructed in these stern doctrines.

We might also ask just how "global" the economy really is, and how much it might be subject to popular democratic control. In terms of trade, financial flows, and other measures, the economy is not more global than early in this century. Furthermore, TNCs rely heavily on public subsidies and domestic markets, and their international transactions, including those mislabeled trade, are largely within Europe, Japan, and the United States, where political measures are available without fear of military coups and the like. There is a great deal that is new and significant, but the belief that things are "out of control" is not very credible, even if we keep to existing mechanisms.

Is it a law of nature that we must keep to these? Not if we take seriously the doctrines of classical liberalism. Adam Smith's praise of division of labor is well known, but not his denunciation of its inhuman effects, which will turn working people into objects "as stupid and ignorant as it is possible for a human creature to be," something that must be prevented "in every improved and civilized society" by government action to overcome the destructive force of the "invisible hand." Also not well advertised is Smith's belief that government "regulation in favour of the workmen is always just and equitable," though not "when in favour of the masters." Or his call for equality of outcome, which was at the heart of his argument for free markets.

Other leading contributors to the classical liberal canon go much further. Wilhelm von Humboldt condemned wage labor itself: when the laborer works under external control, he wrote, "we may admire what he does, but we despise what he is." "The art advances, the artisan recedes," Alexis de Tocqueville observed. Also a great figure of the liberal pantheon, Tocqueville agreed with Smith and Jefferson that equality of outcome is an important feature of a free and just society. One hundred and sixty years ago, he warned of the dangers of a "permanent inequality of conditions" and an end to democracy if "the manufacturing aristocracy which is growing up under our eyes" in the United States, "one of the harshest that has ever existed in the world," should escape its confines—as it later did, beyond his worst nightmares.

I am only barely touching on intricate and fascinating issues, which suggest, I think, that leading principles of classical liberalism receive their natural modern expression not in the neoliberal "religion" but in the independent movements of working people and the ideas and practices of the libertarian socialist movements, at times articulated also by such major figures of twentieth-century thought as Bertrand Russell and John Dewey.

One has to evaluate with caution the doctrines that dominate intellectual discourse, with careful attention to the argument, the facts, and the lessons of past and present history. It makes little sense to ask what is "right" for particular countries as if these are entities with common interests and values. And what may be right for people in the United States, with their unparalleled advantages, could well be wrong for others who have a much narrower scope of choices. We can, however, reasonably anticipate that what is right for the people of the world will only by the remotest accident conform to the plans of the "principal architects" of policy. And there is no more reason now than there ever has been to permit them to shape the future in their own interests.

A version of this article was originally published in South America in Spanish and Portuguese translations, 1996.

II

Consent

without

Consent:

Regimenting the Public Mind

A decent democratic society should be based on the principle of "consent of the governed." That idea has won general acceptance, but it can be challenged as both too strong and too weak. Too strong, because it suggests that people must be governed and controlled. Too weak, because even the most brutal rulers require some measure of "consent of the governed," and generally obtain it, not only by force.

I am interested here in how the more free and democratic societies have dealt with these issues. Over the years, popular forces have sought to gain a larger share in managing their affairs, with some success alongside many defeats. Meanwhile an instructive body of thought has been developed to justify elite resistance to democracy. Those who hope to understand the past and shape the future would do well to pay careful attention not only to the practice but also to the doctrinal framework that supports it.

The issues were addressed 250 years ago by David Hume in classic work. Hume was intrigued by "the easiness with which the many are governed by the few, the implicit submission with which men resign" their fate to their rulers. This he found surprising, because "force is always on the side of the governed." If people would realize that, they would rise up and overthrow the masters. He concluded that government is founded on control of opinion, a principle that "extends to the most despotic and most military governments, as well as to the most free and most popular."

Hume surely underestimated the effectiveness of brute force. A more accurate version is that the more "free and popular" a government, the more it becomes necessary to rely on control of opinion to ensure submission to the rulers.

That people must submit is taken for granted pretty much across the spectrum. In a democracy, the governed have the right to consent, but nothing more than that. In the terminology of modern progressive thought, the population may be "spectators," but not "participants," apart from occasional choices among leaders representing authentic power. That is the political arena. The general population must be excluded entirely from the economic arena, where what happens in the society is largely determined. Here the public is to have no role, according to prevailing democratic theory.

These assumptions have been challenged throughout history, but the issues have taken on particular force since the first modern democratic upsurge in seventeenth century England. The turmoil of the time is often depicted as a conflict between King and Parliament, but as is often true, a good part of the population did not want to be governed by either of the contestants for power but "by countrymen like ourselves, that know our wants," so their pamphlets declared, not by "knights and gentlemen" who do not "know the people's sores" and will "but oppress us."

Such ideas greatly distressed "the men of best quality," as they called themselves: the "responsible men," in modern terminology. They were prepared to grant the people rights, but within limits, and on the principle that by "the people" we do not mean the confused and ignorant rabble. But how is that fundamental principle of social life to be reconciled with the doctrine of "consent of the governed," which was not so easy to suppress by then? A solution to the problem was proposed by Hume's contemporary Frances Hutcheson, a distinguished moral philosopher. He argued that the principle of "consent of the governed" is not violated when the rulers impose plans that are rejected by the public, if later on the "stupid" and "prejudiced" masses "will heartily consent" to what we have done in their name. We can adopt the principle of "consent without consent," the term used later by sociologist Franklin Henry Giddings.

Hutcheson was concerned with control of the rabble at home; Giddings, with enforcing order abroad. He was writing about the Philippines, which the U.S. army was liberating at the time, while also liberating several hundred thousand souls from life's sorrows—or, as the press put it, "slaughtering the natives in English fashion" so that "the misguided creatures" who resist us will at least "respect our arms" and later come to recognize that we wish them "liberty" and "happiness." To explain all of this in properly civilized tones, Giddings devised his concept of "consent without consent": "If in later years, [the conquered people] see and admit that the disputed relation was for the highest interest, it may be reasonably held that authority has been imposed with the consent of the governed," as when a parent prevents a child from running into a busy street.

These explanations capture the real meaning of the doctrine of "consent of the governed." The people must submit to their rulers, and it is enough if they give consent without consent. Within a tyrannical state or in foreign domains, force can be used. When the resources of violence are limited, the consent of the governed must be obtained by the devices called "manufacture of consent" by progressive and liberal opinion.

The enormous public relations industry, from its origins early in this century, has been dedicated to the "control of the public mind," as business leaders described the task. And they acted on their words, surely one of the central themes of modern history. The fact that the public relations industry has its roots and major centers in the country that is "most free" is exactly what we should expect, with a proper understanding of Hume's maxim.

A few years after Hume and Hutcheson wrote, the problems caused by the rabble in England spread to the rebelling colonies of North America. The founding fathers repeated the sentiments of the British "men of best quality" in almost the same words. As one put it: "When I mention the public, I mean to include only the rational part of it. The ignorant and vulgar are as unfit to judge of the modes [of government], as they are unable to manage [its] reins." The people are a "great beast" that must be tamed, his colleague Alexander Hamilton declared. Rebellious and independent farmers had to be taught, sometimes by force, that the ideals of the revolutionary pamphlets were not to be taken too seriously. The common people were not to be represented by countrymen like themselves, who know the people's sores, but by gentry, merchants, lawyers, and other "responsible men" who could be trusted to defend privilege.

The reigning doctrine was expressed clearly by the President of the Continental Congress and first Chief Justice of the Supreme Court, John Jay: "The people who own the country ought to govern it." One issue remained to be settled: Who owns the country? The question was answered by the rise of private corporations and the structures devised to protect and support them, though it remains a difficult task to compel the public to keep to the spectator role.

The United States is surely the most important case to study if we hope to understand the world of today and tomorrow. One reason is its incomparable power. Another is its stable democratic institutions. Furthermore, the United States was as close to a *tabula rasa* as one can find. America can be "as happy as she pleases," Thomas Paine remarked in 1776: "she has a blank sheet to write upon." The indigenous societies were largely eliminated. The U.S. also has little residue of earlier European structures, one reason for the relative weakness of the social contract and of support systems, which often had their roots in precapitalist institutions. And to an unusual extent, the sociopolitical order was consciously designed. In studying history, one cannot construct experiments, but the United States is as close to the "ideal case" of state capitalist democracy as can be found.

The main designer, furthermore, was an astute political thinker: James Madison, whose views largely prevailed. In the debates on the Constitution, Madison pointed out that if elections in England "were open to all classes of people, the property of landed proprietors would be insecure. An agrarian law would soon take place," giving land to the landless. The Constitutional system must be designed to prevent such injustice and "secure the permanent interests of the country," which are property rights.

Among Madisonian scholars, there is a consensus that "the Constitution was intrinsically an aristocratic document designed to check the democratic tendencies of the period," delivering power to a "better sort" of people and excluding those who were not rich, well born, or prominent from exercising political power (Lance Banning). The primary responsibility of government is "to protect the minority of the opulent against the majority," Madison declared. That has been the guiding principle of the democratic system from its origins until today.

In public discussion, Madison spoke of the rights of minorities in general, but it is quite clear that he had a particular minority in mind: "the minority of the opulent." Modern political theory stresses Madison's belief that "in a just and a free government the rights both of property and of persons ought to be effectually guarded." But in this case too it is useful to look at the doctrine more carefully. There are no rights *of* property, only rights *to* property: that is, rights of persons with property. Perhaps I have a right to my car, but my car has no rights. The right to property also differs from others in that one person's possession of property deprives another of that right: if I own my car, you do not; but in a just and free society, my freedom of speech would not limit yours. The Madisonian principle, then, is that government must guard the rights of persons generally, but must provide special and additional guarantees for the rights of one class of persons, property owners.

Madison foresaw that the threat of democracy was likely to become more severe over time because of the increase in "the proportion of those who will labor under all the hardships of life, and secretly sigh for a more equal distribution of its blessings." They might gain influence, Madison feared. He was concerned by the "symptoms of a leveling spirit" that had already appeared, and warned "of the future danger" if the right to vote would place "power over property in hands without a share in it." Those "without property, or the hope of acquiring it, cannot be expected to sympathize sufficiently with its rights," Madison explained. His solution was to keep political power in the hands of those who "come from and represent the wealth of the nation," the "more capable set of men," with the general public fragmented and disorganized.

The problem of a "leveling spirit" also arises abroad, of course. We learn a lot about "really existing democratic theory" by seeing how this problem is perceived, particularly in secret internal documents, where leaders can be more frank and open.

Take the important example of Brazil, the "colossus of the South." On a visit in 1960, President Eisenhower assured Brazilians that "our socially conscious private-enterprise system benefits all the people, owners and workers alike... In freedom the Brazilian worker is happily demonstrating the joys of life under a democratic system." The ambassador added that U.S. influence had broken "down the old order in South America" by bringing to it "such revolutionary ideas as free compulsory education, equality before the law, a relatively classless society, a responsible democratic system of government, free competitive enterprise, [and] a fabulous standard of living for the masses."

But Brazilians reacted harshly to the good news brought by their northern tutors. Latin American elites are "like children," Secretary of State John Foster Dulles informed the National Security Council, "with practically no capacity for self-government." Worse still, the United States is "hopelessly far behind the Soviets in developing controls over the minds and emotions of unsophisticated peoples." Dulles and Eisenhower expressed their concern over the Communist "ability to get control of mass movements," an ability that "we have no capacity to duplicate": "The poor people are the ones they appeal to and they have always wanted to plunder the rich."

In other words, we find it hard to induce people to accept our doctrine that the rich should plunder the poor, a public relations problem that had not yet been solved.

The Kennedy Administration faced the problem by shifting the mission of the Latin American military from "hemispheric defense" to "internal security," a decision with fateful consequences, beginning with the brutal and murderous military coup in Brazil. The military had been seen by Washington as an "island of sanity" in Brazil, and the coup was welcomed by Kennedy's ambassador, Lincoln Gordon, as a "democratic rebellion," indeed "the single most decisive victory of freedom in the mid-twentieth century." A former Harvard University economist, Gordon added that this "victory of freedom"—that is, the violent overthrow of parliamentary democracy—should "create a greatly improved climate for private investments," giving some further insight into the operative meaning of the terms *freedom* and *democracy*.

Two years later Defense Secretary Robert McNamara informed his associates that "U.S. policies toward the Latin American military have, on the whole, been effective in attaining the goals set for them." These policies had improved "internal security capabilities" and established "predominant U.S. military influence." The Latin American military understand their tasks and are equipped to pursue them, thanks to Kennedy's programs of military aid and training. These tasks include the overthrow of civilian governments "whenever, in the judgment of the military, the conduct of these leaders is injurious to the welfare of the nation." Such actions by the military are necessary in "the Latin American cultural environment," the Kennedy intellectuals explained. And we can be confident that they will be carried out properly, now that the military have gained an "understanding of, and orientation toward, U.S. objectives." That assures a proper outcome to the "revolutionary struggle for power among major groups which constitute the present class structure" in Latin America, an outcome that will protect "private U.S. investment" and trade, the "economic root" that is at the heart of "U.S. political interest in Latin America."

These are secret documents; in this case, of Kennedy liberalism. Public discourse is naturally quite different. If we keep to it, we will understand little about the true meaning of "democracy," or about the global order of the past years; and the future as well, since the same hands hold the reins.

The more serious scholarship is clear about the basic facts. The National Security States installed and backed by the United States are discussed in an important book by Lars Schoultz, one of the leading Latin American scholars. Their goal, in his words, was "to destroy permanently a perceived threat to the existing structure of socioeconomic privilege by eliminating the political participation of the numerical majority," Hamilton's "great beast." The goal is basically the same in the home society, though the means are different.

The pattern continues today. The champion human rights violator in the hemisphere is Colombia, also the leading recipient of U.S. military aid and training in recent years. The pretext is the "drug war," but that is "a myth," as regularly reported by major human rights groups, the church, and other who have investigated the shocking record of atrocities and the close links between the narcotraffickers, landowners, the military, and their paramilitary associates. State terror has devastated popular organizations and virtually destroyed the one independent political party by assassination of thousands of activists, including presidential candidates, mayors, and others. Nonetheless Colombia is hailed as a stable democracy, revealing again what is meant by "democracy."

A particularly instructive example is the reaction to Guatemala's first experiment with democracy. In this case the secret record is partially available, so we know a good deal about the thinking that guided policy. In 1952 the CIA warned that the "radical and nationalist policies" of the government had gained "the support or acquiescence of almost all Guatemalans." The government was "mobilizing the hitherto politically inert peasantry" and creating "mass support for the present regime" by means of labor organization, agrarian reform, and other policies "identified with the revolution of 1944," which had aroused "a strong national movement to free Guatemala from the military dictatorship, social backwardness, and 'economic colonialism' which had been the pattern of the past." The policies of the democratic government "inspired the loyalty and conformed to the self-interest of most politically conscious Guatemalans." State Department intelligence reported that the democratic leadership "insisted upon the maintenance of an open political system," thus allowing Communists to "expand their operations and appeal effectively to various sectors of the population." These deficiencies of democracy were cured by the military coup of 1954 and the reign of terror since, always with large-scale U.S. support.

The problem of securing "consent" has also arisen with international institutions. At first, the United Nations was a reliable instrument of U.S. policy, and was greatly admired. But decolonization brought about what came to be called "the tyranny of the majority." From the 1960s Washington took the lead in vetoing Security Council resolutions (with Britain second, and France a distant third), and voting alone or with a few client states against General Assembly resolutions. The UN fell into disfavor, and sober articles began to appear asking why the world was "opposing the United States"; that the United States might be opposing the world is a thought too bizarre to be entertained. U.S. relations with the World Court and other international institutions have undergone a similar evolution, to which we return.

My comments on the Madisonian roots of the prevailing concepts of democracy were unfair in an important respect. Like Adam Smith and other founders of classical liberalism, Madison was precapitalist, and anticapitalist in spirit. He expected that the rulers would be "enlightened Statesmen" and "benevolent philosophers," "whose wisdom may best discern the true interests of their country." They would "refine" and "enlarge" the "public views," guarding the true interests of the country against the "mischiefs" of democratic majorities, but with enlightenment and benevolence.

Madison soon learned differently, as the "opulent minority" proceeded to use their newfound power much as Adam Smith had predicted a few years earlier. They were intent on pursuing what Smith called the "vile maxim" of the masters: "All for ourselves, and nothing for other people." By 1792 Madison warned that the rising developmental capitalist state was "substituting the motive of private interest in place of public duty," leading to "a real domination of the few under an apparent liberty of the many." He deplored "the daring depravity of the times," as private powers "become the pretorian band of the government—at once its tools and its tyrant; bribed by its largesses, and overawing it by clamors and combinations." They cast over society the shadow that we call "politics," as John Dewey later commented. One of the major twentieth century philosophers and a leading figure of North American liberalism, Dewey emphasized that democracy has little content when big business rules the life of the country through its control of "the means of production, exchange, publicity, transportation and communication, reinforced by command of the press, press agents and other means of publicity and propaganda." He held further that in a free and democratic society, workers must be "the masters of their own industrial fate," not tools rented by employers, ideas that can be traced back to classical liberalism and the Enlightenment, and have constantly reappeared in popular struggle in the United States as elsewhere.

There have been many changes in the past 200 years, but Madison's words of warning have only become more appropriate, taking new meaning with the establishment of great private tyrannies that were granted extraordinary powers early in this century, primarily by the courts. The theories devised to justify these "collectivist legal entities," as they are sometimes called by legal historians, are based on ideas that also underlie fascism and Bolshevism: that organic entities have rights over and above those of persons. They receive ample "largesses" from the states they largely dominate, remaining both "tools and tyrants," in Madison's phrase. And they have gained substantial control over the domestic and international economy as well as the informational and doctrinal systems, bringing to mind another of Madison's concerns: that "a popular Government, without popular information, or the means of acquiring it, is but a Prologue to a Farce or a Tragedy; or perhaps both."

Let's now look at the doctrines that have been crafted to impose the modern forms of political democracy. They are expressed quite accurately in an important manual of the public relations industry by one of its leading figures, Edward Bernays. He opens by observing that "the conscious and intelligent manipulation of the organized habits and opinions of the masses is an important element in democratic society." To carry out this essential task, "the intelligent minorities must make use of propaganda continuously and systematically," because they alone "understand the mental processes and social patterns of the masses" and can "pull the wires which control the public mind." Therefore, our "society has consented to permit free competition to be organized by leadership and propaganda," another case of "consent without consent." Propaganda provides the leadership with a mechanism "to mold the mind of the masses" so that "they will throw their newly gained strength in the desired direction." The leadership can "regiment the public mind every bit as much as an army regiments the bodies of its soldiers." This process of "engineering consent" is the very "essence of the democratic process," Bernays wrote shortly before he was honored for his contributions by the American Psychological Association in 1949.

The importance of "controlling the public mind" has been recognized with increasing clarity as popular struggles succeeded in extending the modalities of democracy, thus giving rise to what liberal elites call "the crisis of democracy" as when normally passive and apathetic populations become organized and seek to enter the political arena to pursue their interests and demands, threatening stability and order. As Bernays explained the problem, with "universal suffrage and universal schooling…at last even the bourgeoisie stood in fear of the common people. For the masses promised to become king," a tendency fortunately reversed—so it has been hoped—as new methods "to mold the mind of the masses" were devised and implemented.

A good New Deal liberal, Bernays had developed his skills in Woodrow Wilson's Committee on Public Information, the first U.S. state propaganda agency. "It was the astounding success of propaganda during the war that opened the eyes of the intelligent few in all departments of life to the possibilities of regimenting the public mind," Bernays explained in his public relations manual, entitled "Propaganda." The intelligent few were perhaps unaware that their "astounding success" relied in no small part on propaganda fabrications about Hun atrocities provided to them by the British Ministry of Information, which secretly defined its task as "to direct the thought of most of the world."

All of this is good Wilsonian doctrine, known as "Wilsonian idealism" in political theory. Wilson's own view was that an elite of gentlemen with "elevated ideals" is needed to preserve "stability and righteousness." It is the intelligent minority of "responsible men" who must control decision making, another veteran of Wilson's propaganda committee, Walter Lippmann, explained in his influential essays on democracy. Lippmann was also the most respected figure in U.S. journalism and a noted commentator on public affairs for half a century. The intelligent minority are a "specialized class" who are responsible for setting policy and for "the formation of a sound public opinion," Lippmann elaborated. They must be free from interference by the general public, who are "ignorant and meddlesome outsiders." The public must "be put in its place," Lippmann continued: their "function" is to be "spectators of action," not participants, apart from periodic electoral exercises when they choose among the specialized class. Leaders must be free to operate in "technocratic insulation," to borrow current World Bank terminology.

In the *Encyclopaedia of the Social Sciences*, Harold Lasswell, one of the founders of modern political science, warned that the intelligent few must recognize the "ignorance and stupidity of the masses" and not succumb to "democratic dogmatisms about men being the best judges of their own interests." They are not the best judges; we are. The masses must be controlled for their own good, and in more democratic societies, where force is unavailable, social managers must turn to "a whole new technique of control, largely through propaganda."

Note that this is good Leninist doctrine. The similarity between progressive democratic theory and Marxism-Leninism is rather striking, something that Bakunin had predicted long before.

With a proper understanding of the concept of "consent," we can see that implementation of the business agenda over the objections of the general public is "with the consent of the governed," a form of "consent without consent." That is a fair description of what has been happening in the United States. There is often a gap between public preferences and public policy. In recent years the gap has become substantial. A comparison sheds further light on the functioning of the democratic system.

More than 80 percent of the public think that the government is "run for the benefit of the few and the special interests, not the people," up from about 50 percent in earlier years. Over 80 percent believe that the economic system is "inherently unfair," and that working people have too little say in what goes on in the country. More than 70 percent feel that "business has gained too much power over too many aspects of American life." And by almost 20 to 1, the public believe that corporations "should sometimes sacrifice some profit for the sake of making things better for their workers and communities."

Public attitudes remain stubbornly social democratic in important respects, as they did through the Reagan years, contrary to a good deal of mythology. But we should also note that these attitudes fall far short of the ideas that animated the democratic revolutions. Working people of nineteenth century North America did not plead with their rulers to be more benevolent. Rather, they denied their right to rule. "Those who work in the mills should own them," the labor press demanded, upholding the ideals of the American revolution as the dangerous rabble understood them.

The 1994 congressional election is a revealing example of the gap between rhetoric and fact. It was called a "political earthquake," a "landslide victory," a "triumph of conservatism" that reflects the continuing "drift to the right" as voters gave an "overwhelming popular mandate" to Newt Gingrich's ultraright army, who promised to "get government off our backs" and bring back the happy days when the free market reigned.

Turning to the facts, the "landslide victory" was won with barely more than half the votes cast, about 20 percent of the electorate, figures that hardly differ from two years earlier, when the Democrats won. One out of six voters described the outcome as "an affirmation of the Republican agenda." One out of four had heard of the Contract with America, which presented that agenda. And when informed, the population opposed virtually all of it by large majorities. About 60 percent of the public wanted social spending *increased*. A year later, 80 percent held that "the federal government must protect the most vulnerable in society, especially the poor and the elderly, by guaranteeing minimum living standards and providing social benefits." Eighty to 90 percent of Americans support federal guarantees of public assistance for those who cannot work, unemployment insurance, subsidized prescription drugs and nursing home care for the elderly, a minimum level of health care, and social security. Three-quarters support federally guaranteed child care for low-income working mothers. The resilience of such attitudes is particularly striking in the light of the unremitting propaganda assault to persuade the public that they hold radically different beliefs.

Public opinion studies show that the more voters learned about the Republican program in Congress, the more they opposed the party and its congressional program. The standard-bearer of the revolution, Newt Gingrich, was unpopular at the time of his "triumph," and sank steadily afterward, becoming perhaps the most unpopular political figure in the country. One of the more comical aspects of the 1996 elections was the scene of Gingrich's closest associates struggling to deny any connection to their leader and his ideas. In the primaries the first candidate to disappear, virtually at once, was Phil Gramm, the sole representative of the congressional Republicans, very well funded and saying all the words that the voters are supposed to love, according to the headlines. In fact, almost the full range of policy issues disappeared instantly as soon as the candidates had to face the voters in January 1996. The most dramatic example was balancing the budget. Through 1995, the major issue in the country was how quickly to do it, seven years or a bit longer. The government was shut down several times as the controversy raged. As soon as the primaries opened, talk of the budget was gone. The *Wall Street Journal* reported with surprise that voters "have abandoned their balanced-budget obsession." The actual "obsession" of the voters was precisely the opposite, as polls had regularly shown: their opposition to balancing the budget under any minimally realistic assumptions.

To be accurate, parts of the public did share the "obsession" of both political parties with balancing the budget. In August 1995 the deficit was chosen as the country's most important problem by 5 percent of the population, ranking alongside homelessness. But the 5 percent who were obsessed with the budget happened to include people who matter. "American business has spoken: balance the federal budget," *Business Week* announced, reporting a poll of senior executives. And when business speaks, so do the political class and the media, which informed the public that it demanded a balanced budget, detailing the cuts in social spending in accord with the public will—and over its substantial opposition, as polls demonstrated. It is not surprising that the topic suddenly disappeared from view as soon as politicians had to face the great beast.

It is also not surprising that the agenda continues to be implemented in its standard double-edged fashion, with cruel and often unpopular cuts in social spending alongside increases in the

Pentagon budget that the public opposes, but with strong business support in both cases. The reasons for the spending increases are easily understood when we bear in mind the domestic role of the Pentagon system: to transfer public funds to advanced sectors of industry, so that Newt Gingrich's rich constituents, for example, can be protected from the rigors of the marketplace with more government subsidies than any other suburban district in the country (outside the federal government itself), while the leader of the conservative revolution denounces big government and lauds rugged individualism.

From the beginning it was clear from the polls that the stories about the conservative landslide were untrue. Now the fraud is quietly conceded. The polling specialist of the Gingrich Republicans explained that when he reported that most people supported the Contract with America, what he meant was that they liked the slogans that were used for packaging. For example, his studies showed that the public opposes dismantling the health system and wants to "preserve, protect and strengthen" it "for the next generation." So dismantling is packaged as "a solution that preserves and protects" the health system for the next generation. The same is true generally.

All of this is very natural in a society that is, to an unusual degree, business-run, with huge expenditures on marketing: $1 trillion a year, one-sixth of gross domestic product, much of it tax-deductible, so that people pay for the privilege of being subjected to manipulation of their attitudes and behavior.

But the great beast is hard to tame. Repeatedly it has been thought that the problem has been solved, and that the "end of history" has been reached in a kind of utopia of the masters. One classic moment was at the origins of neoliberal doctrine in the early nineteenth century, when David Ricardo, Thomas Malthus, and other great figures of classical economics announced that the new science had proven, with the certainty of Newton's laws, that we only harm the poor by trying to help them, and that the best gift we can offer the suffering masses is to free them from the delusion that they have a right to live. The new science proved that people had no rights beyond what they can obtain in the unregulated labor market. By the 1830s it seemed that these doctrines had won the day in England. With the triumph of right thinking at the service of British manufacturing and financial interests, the people of England were "forced into the paths of a utopian experiment," Karl Polanyi wrote in his classic work, *The Great Transformation*, fifty years ago. It was the most "ruthless act of social reform" in all of history, he continued, which "crushed multitudes of lives." But an unanticipated problem arose. The stupid masses began to draw the conclusion that if we have no right to live, then you have no right to rule. The British army had to cope with riots and disorder, and soon an even greater threat took shape as workers began to organize, demanding factory laws and social legislation to protect them from the harsh neoliberal experiment, and often going well beyond. The science, which is fortunately flexible, took new forms as elite opinion shifted in response to uncontrollable popular forces, discovering that the right to live had to be preserved under a social contract of sorts.

Later in the century, it seemed to many that order had been restored, though a few dissented. The famous artist William Morris outraged respectable opinion by declaring himself a socialist in a talk at Oxford. He recognized that it was "the received opinion that the competitive or 'Devil take the hindmost' system is the last system of economy which the world will see; that it is perfection, and therefore finality has been reached in it." But if history really is at an end, he continued, then "civilization will die." And this he refused to believe, despite the confident proclamations of "the most learned men." He was right, as popular struggle demonstrated.

In the United States too, the Gay Nineties a century ago were hailed as "perfection" and "finality." And by the Roaring Twenties, it was confidently assumed that labor had been crushed for good, and the utopia of the masters achieved—in "a most undemocratic America" that was "created over its workers' protests," Yale

University historian David Montgomery comments. But again the celebration was premature. Within a few years the great beast once again escaped its cage, and even the United States, the business-run society par excellence, was forced by popular struggle to grant rights that had long ago been won in far more autocratic societies.

Immediately after World War II, business launched a huge propaganda offensive to regain what it had lost. By the late 1950s it was widely assumed that the goal had been achieved. We had reached the "end of ideology" in the industrial world, Harvard sociologist Daniel Bell wrote. A few years earlier, as an editor of the leading business journal *Fortune*, he had reported the "staggering" scale of business propaganda campaigns designed to overcome the social democratic attitudes that persisted into the postwar years.

But again the celebration was premature. Events of the 1960s showed that the great beast was still on the prowl, once again arousing the fear of democracy among "responsible men." The Trilateral Commission, founded by David Rockefeller in 1973, devoted its first major study to the "crisis of democracy" throughout the industrial world as large sectors of the population sought to enter the public arena. The naive might think of that as a step toward democracy, but the Commission understood that it was "excessive democracy," and hoped to restore the days when "Truman had been able to govern the country with the cooperation of a relatively small number of Wall Street lawyers and bankers," as the American rapporteur commented. That was proper "moderation in democracy." Of particular concern to the Commission were the failures of what it called the institutions responsible "for the indoctrination of the young": the schools, universities, and churches. The Commission proposed means to restore discipline, and to return the general public to passivity and obedience, overcoming the crisis of democracy.

The Commission represents the more progressive internationalist sectors of power and intellectual life in the United States, Europe, and Japan: the Carter Administration was drawn almost entirely from its ranks. The right wing takes a much harsher line.

From the 1970s, changes in the international economy

have put new weapons into the hands of the masters, enabling them to chip away at the hated social contract that had been won by popular struggle. The political spectrum in the United States, always very narrow, has been reduced to near invisibility. A few months after Bill Clinton took office, the lead story in the *Wall Street Journal* expressed its pleasure that "on issue after issue, Mr. Clinton and his administration come down on the same side as corporate America," eliciting cheers from heads of major corporations, who were delighted that "we're getting along much better with this administration than we did with previous ones," as one put it.

A year later, business leaders found they could do even better, and by September 1995 *Business Week* reported that the new Congress "represents a milestone for business: Never before have so many goodies been showered so enthusiastically on America's entrepreneurs." In the November 1996 elections, both candidates were moderate Republicans and longtime government insiders, candidates of the business world. The campaign was one of "historic dullness," the business press reported. Polls showed that public interest had declined even below the previous low levels despite record-breaking spending, and that voters disliked both candidates and expected little from either of them.

There is large-scale discontent with the workings of the democratic system. A similar phenomenon has been reported in Latin America, and though conditions are quite different, some of the reasons are the same. Argentine political scientist Atilio Boron has stressed the fact that in Latin America, the democratic process was established together with neoliberal economic reforms, which have been a disaster for most people. The introduction of similar programs in the richest country in the world has had similar effects. When more than 80 percent of the population feel that the democratic system is a sham and that the economy is "inherently unfair," "the consent of the governed" is going to be very shallow.

The business press records "capital's clear subjugation of labor for the past 15 years," which has allowed it to win many victories. But it also warns that the glorious days may not last because of the increasingly "aggressive campaign" of workers "to secure a so-called 'living wage'" and "a guaranteed bigger piece of the pie."

It is worth remembering that we have been through all of this before. The "end of history," "perfection," and "finality" have often been proclaimed, always falsely. And with all the sordid continuities, an optimistic soul can still discern slow progress, realistically, I think. In the advanced industrial countries, and often elsewhere too, popular struggles can start from a higher plane and with greater expectations than those of the Gay Nineties and Roaring Twenties, or even thirty years ago. And international solidarity can take new and more constructive forms as the great majority of the people of the world come to understand that their interests are pretty much the same and can be advanced by working together. There is no more reason now than there has ever been to believe that we are constrained by mysterious and unknown social laws, not simply decisions made within institutions that are subject to human will—*human* institutions, that have to face the test of legitimacy and, if they do not meet it, can be replaced by others that are more free and more just, as often in the past.

A version of this article was originally published in South America in Spanish and Portuguese translations, 1996.

III

The **Passion**
for
Free Markets

"For more than half a century, the United Nations has been the main forum for the United States to try to create a world in its image, maneuvering with its allies to forge global accords about human rights, nuclear tests, or the environment that Washington insisted would mirror its own values." So runs postwar history, we learn from the opening paragraph of a front-page story by *New York Times* political analyst David Sanger. But times are changing. Today, the headline reads, "U.S. Is Exporting Its Free-Market Values through Global Commercial Agreements." Going beyond the traditional reliance on the UN, the Clinton Administration is turning to the new World Trade Organization (WTO) to carry out the task of "exporting American values." Down the road, Sanger continues (quoting the U.S. trade representative), it is the WTO that may be the most effective instrument for bringing "America's passion for deregulation" and for the free market generally, and "the American values of free competition, fair rules, and effective enforcement," to a world still fumbling in darkness. These "American values" are illustrated most dramatically by the wave of the future: telecommunications, the Internet, advanced computer technology, and the other wonders created by the exuberant American entrepreneurial spirit unleashed by the market, at last freed from government interference by the Reagan revolution.

Today "governments are everywhere embracing the free-market gospel preached in the 1980s by President Reagan and Prime Minister Margaret Thatcher of Britain," Youssef Ibrahim reports in another *Times* front-page story, reiterating a common theme. Like it or hate it, enthusiasts and critics over a broad range of opinion agree—just to keep to the liberal-to-left part of the spectrum—about "the implacable sweep of what its exponents call 'the market revolution'": "Reaganesque rugged individualism" has changed the rules of the game worldwide, while here at home "Republicans and Democrats alike are ready to give the market full sway" in their dedication to "the new orthodoxy."[1]

There are a number of problems with the picture. One is the account of the last half-century. Even the most dedicated believers in "America's mission" must be aware that U.S.-UN relations have been virtually the opposite of what the opening passage depicts ever since the UN fell out of control with the progress of decolonization, leaving the United States regularly isolated in opposition to global accords on a wide range of issues and committed to undermining central components of the UN, particularly those with a third world orientation. Many questions about the world are debatable, but surely not this one.

As for "Reaganesque rugged individualism" and its worship of the market, perhaps it is enough to quote the review of the Reagan years in *Foreign Affairs* by a senior fellow for international finance at the Council on Foreign Relations, noting the "irony" that Ronald Reagan, "the postwar chief executive with the most passionate love of laissez faire, presided over the greatest swing toward protectionism since the 1930s"[2]—no "irony," but the normal workings of "passionate love of laissez-faire": for *you*, market discipline, but not for *me*, unless the "playing field" happens to be tilted in my favor, typically as a result of large-scale state intervention. It is hard to find another theme so dominant in the economic history of the past three centuries.

Reaganites were following a well-trodden course—recently turned into a comedy act by Gingrich "conservatives"—when they extolled the glories of the market and issued stern lectures about the debilitating culture of dependency to the poor at home and abroad while boasting proudly to the business world that Reagan had "granted more import relief to U.S. industry than any of his predecessors in more than half a century"; in fact, more than all predecessors combined, as they led "the sustained assault on [free trade] principle" by the rich and powerful from the early 1970s deplored in a scholarly review by General Agreement on Tariffs and Trade (GATT) secretariat economist Patrick Low, who estimates the restrictive effects of Reaganite measures at about three times those of other leading industrial countries.[3]

The radical "swing toward protectionism" was only a part of the "sustained assault" on free trade principles that was accelerated under "Reaganite rugged individualism." Another chapter of the story includes the huge transfer of public funds to private power, often under the traditional guise of "security." The centuries-old tale proceeds today without notable change; not only here, of course, though new heights of deception and hypocrisy may have been scaled on the local terrain.

"Thatcher's Britain" is, in fact, another good choice to illustrate "free market gospel." Just to keep to a few revelations of the past few months (early 1997), "during the period of maximum pressure to make arms sales to Turkey," the London *Observer* reported, Prime Minister Thatcher "personally intervened to ensure a payment of £22m was made out of Britain's overseas aid budget, to help build a metro in the Turkish capital of Ankara. The project was uneconomical, and in 1995 it was admitted" by Foreign Secretary Douglas Hurd that it was "unlawful." The incident was particularly noteworthy in the aftermath of the Pergau Dam scandal, which revealed illegal Thatcherite subsidies "to 'sweeten' arms deals with the Malaysian regime," with a High Court judgment against Hurd. That's aside from government credit guarantees and financing arrangements, and the rest of the panoply of devices to transfer public funds to the "defense industry," yielding a familiar range of benefits to advanced industry generally.

A few days before, the same journal reported that "up to 2 million British children are suffering ill-health and stunted growth because of malnutrition" as a result of "poverty on a scale not seen since the 1930s." The trend to increasing child health has reversed, and childhood diseases that had been controlled are now on the upswing thanks to the (highly selective) "free market gospel" that is much admired by its beneficiaries.

A few months earlier, a lead headline reported "One in Three British Babies Born in Poverty," as "child poverty has increased as much as three-fold since Margaret Thatcher was elected." "Dickensian Diseases Return to Haunt Today's Britain," another headline reads, reporting studies concluding that "social conditions in Britain are returning to those of a century ago." Particularly grim are the effects of cutting off gas, electricity, water, and telephones to "a high number of households" as privatization takes its natural course, with a variety of devices that favor "more affluent customers" and amount to a "surcharge on the poor," leading to a "growing gulf in energy between rich and poor," also in water supply and other services. The "savage cuts" in social programs are placing the nation "in the grip of panic about imminent social collapse." But industry and finance are benefiting very nicely from the same policy choices. And to top it all off, public spending after seventeen years of Thatcherite gospel was the same 42.25 percent of GDP that it was when she took over.[4]

Not exactly unfamiliar here.

The World Trade Organization: "Exporting American Values"

Let us put aside the intriguing contrast between doctrine and reality, and see what can be learned by examining the new era that is coming into view. Quite a lot, I think.

The *Times* story on how the "U.S. is exporting its free-market values" is celebrating the WTO agreement on telecommunications. One of its welcome effects is to provide Washington with a "new tool of foreign policy." The agreement "empowers the WTO to go inside the borders of the 70 countries that have signed it," and it is no secret that international institutions can function insofar as they keep to the demands of the powerful, in particular, the United States. In the real world, then, the "new tool" allows the United States to intervene profoundly in the internal affairs of others, compelling them to change their laws and practices. Crucially, the WTO will make sure that other countries are "following through on their commitments to allow foreigners to invest" without restriction in central areas of their economy. In the specific case at hand, the likely outcome is clear to all: "The obvious corporate beneficiaries of this new era will be U.S. carriers, who are best positioned to dominate a level playing field," the *Far Eastern Economic Review* points out,[5] along with one U.K.-U.S. megacorporation.

Not everyone is delighted by the prospects. The winners recognize that fact, and offer their interpretation: in Sanger's words, others fear that "American telecommunication giants...could overwhelm the flabby government-sanctioned monopolies that have long dominated telecommunications in Europe and Asia"—as in the United States, long past the period when it had become by far the world's leading economy and most powerful state. It is also worth noting that major contributions to modern technology (transistors, to mention just one) came from the research laboratories of the "flabby government-sanctioned monopoly" that dominated telecommunications here until the 1970s. It used its freedom from market discipline to provide for the needs of advanced sectors of industry generally by transfer of public funds (sometimes in indirect ways, through monopoly power, unlike the more direct modalities of the Pentagon system).

Those who cling irrationally to the past see matters a bit differently. The *Far Eastern Economic Review* points out that jobs will be lost in Asia, and "many Asian consumers will have to pay more for phone service before they will pay less." When will they pay less? For that bright future to dawn, it is only necessary for foreign investors to be "encouraged...to act in socially desired ways," not simply with an eye to profit and service to the rich and the business world. How this miracle will come to pass is unexplained, though doubtless the suggestion will inspire serious reflection in corporate headquarters.

In the time span relevant to planning, the WTO agreement will raise phone service costs for most Asian consumers, the *Review* predicts. "The fact is, comparatively few customers in Asia stand to benefit from cheaper overseas rates" that are anticipated with the takeover by huge foreign corporations, mostly American. In Indonesia, for example, only about 300,000 of some 200 million people—specifically the business sector—make overseas calls at all. "It's very likely the cost of local telecoms service, in general, will rise" in Asia, according to David Barden, regional telecoms analyst at J. P. Morgan Securities in Hong Kong. But that is all to the good, he continues: "If there is no profitability in the business, there will be no business." And now that still more public property is being handed over to foreign corporations, they had better be guaranteed profitability—telecommunications today, and a far wider range of related services tomorrow. The business press predicts that "personal communications over the Internet [including corporate networks and interactions] will overtake telecommunications in five or six years, and telephone operators have the biggest interest in getting into the online business." Contemplating the future of his own company, Intel CEO Andrew Grove sees the Internet as "the biggest change in our environment" at present. He expects large-scale growth for "the connection providers, the people involved in generating the World Wide Web, the people who make the computers" ("people" meaning corporations), and the advertising industry, already running at almost $350 billion annually and anticipating new opportunities with the privatization of the Internet, which is expected to convert it to a global oligopoly.[6]

Meanwhile privatization precedes apace elsewhere. To take one important case, over considerable popular opposition the government of Brazil has decided to privatize the Vale Company, which controls vast uranium, iron, and other mineral resources and industrial and transport facilities, including sophisticated technology. Vale is highly profitable, with a 1996 income of over $5 billion, and excellent prospects for the future; it is one of six Latin American enterprises ranked among the 500 most profitable in the world. A study by specialists of the Graduate School of Engineering at the Federal University in Rio estimated that the government has seriously undervalued the company, noting also that it relied on an "independent" analysis by Merrill Lynch, which happens to be associated with the Anglo-American conglomerate that is seeking to take over this central component of Brazil's economy. The government angrily denies the conclusions. If they are accurate, it will fall into a very familiar pattern.[7]

Side comment: communications are not quite the same as uranium. Concentration of communications in any hands (particularly foreign hands) raises some rather serious questions about meaningful democracy. Similar questions arise about concentration of finance, which undermines popular involvement in social and economic planning. Control over food raises even more serious questions, in this case about survival. A year ago the secretary-general of the UN Food and Agricultural Organization (FAO), discussing the "food crisis following huge rises in cereals prices this year," warned that countries "must become more self-reliant in food production."[8] The FAO is warning "developing countries" to reverse the policies imposed on them by the "Washington consensus," policies that have had a disastrous impact on much of the world, while proving a great boon to subsidized agribusiness—incidentally also to narcotrafficking, perhaps the most dramatic success of neoliberal reforms as judged by the "free market values" that the "U.S. is exporting."

Control over food supplies by foreign corporate giants is well underway, and with the agreement on telecommunications signed and delivered, financial services are next in line.

Summarizing, the expected consequences of the victory for "American values" at the WTO are:

1. A "new tool" for far-reaching U.S. intervention into the internal affairs of others;

2. The takeover of a crucial sector of foreign economies by U.S.-based corporations;

3. Benefits for business sectors and the wealthy;

4. Shifting of costs to the general population;

5. New and potentially powerful weapons against the threat of democracy.

A rational person might ask whether these expectations have something to do with the celebration, or whether they are just incidental to a victory of principle that is celebrated out of commitment to higher values. Skepticism is heightened by comparison of the *Times* picture of the postwar era, cited at the outset, with uncontested fact. It is further enhanced by a look at some of history's striking regularities: among them, that those in a position to impose their projects not only hail them with enthusiasm but also typically benefit from them, whether the values professed involve free trade or other grand principles, which turn out in practice to be finely tuned to the needs of those running the game and cheering the outcome. Logic alone would suggest a touch of skepticism when the pattern is repeated. History should raise it a notch higher.

In fact, we need not even search that far.

The World Trade Organization: An Improper Forum

The same day that the front page was reporting the victory for American values at the WTO, *New York Times* editors warned the European Union not to turn to the WTO to rule on its charge that the U.S. is violating free trade agreements. Narrowly at issue is the Helms-Burton Act, which "compels the United States to impose sanctions against foreign companies that do business in Cuba." The sanctions "would effectively exclude these firms from exporting to, or doing business in, the United States, even if their products and activities have nothing to do with Cuba" (Peter Morici, former director of economics at the U.S. International Trade Commission). That is no slight penalty, even apart from more direct threats against individuals and companies who cross a line that Washington will draw unilaterally. The editors regard the act as a "misguided attempt by Congress to impose its foreign policy on others"; Morici opposes it because it "is creating more costs than benefits" for the United States. More broadly at issue is the embargo itself, "the American economic strangulation of Cuba" that the editors term "a cold war anachronism," best abandoned because it is becoming harmful to U.S. business interests.[9]

But broader questions of right and wrong do not arise, and the whole affair is "essentially a political dispute," the *Times* editors stress, not touching on Washington's "free-trade obligations." Like most others, the editors apparently assume that if Europe persists, the WTO is likely to rule against the United States. Accordingly, the WTO is not a proper forum.

The logic is simple, and standard. Ten years earlier, on the same grounds, the International Court of Justice (ICJ) was found to be an inappropriate forum for judging Nicaragua's charges against Washington. The United States rejected ICJ jurisdiction, and when the court condemned the U.S. for the "unlawful use of force," ordering Washington to cease its international terrorism, violation of treaties, and illegal economic warfare, and to pay substantial reparations, the Democrat-controlled Congress reacted by instantly escalating the crimes while the Court was roundly denounced on all sides as a "hostile forum" that had discredited itself by rendering a decision against the United States. The Court judgment itself was scarcely reported, including the words just quoted and the explicit ruling that U.S. aid to the contras is "military" and not "humanitarian." Along with U.S. direction of the terrorist forces, the aid continued until the United States imposed its will, always called "humanitarian aid." Public history keeps to the same conventions.

The United States then vetoed a Security Council resolution calling on all states to observe international law (scarcely reported), and voted alone (with El Salvador and Israel) against a General Assembly resolution calling for "full and immediate compliance" with the Court's ruling—unreported in the mainstream, as was the repetition the following year, this time with only Israel on board. The whole affair happens to be a typical illustration of how the United States used the UN as a "forum" for imposing its own values (see opening quote).

Returning to the current WTO case, in November 1996 Washington voted alone (with Israel and Uzbekistan) against a General Assembly resolution, backed by the entire European Union(EU), urging the United States to drop the embargo against Cuba. The Organization of American States (OAS) had already voted unanimously to reject the Helms-Burton Act, and had asked its judicial body (the Inter-American Juridical Committee) to rule on its legality. In August 1996 the IAJC ruled unanimously that the act violated international law. A year earlier, the Inter-American Commission on Human Rights of the OAS had condemned U.S. restrictions on shipments of food and medicine to Cuba as a violation of international law. The Clinton Administration's response was that shipments of medicine are not literally barred, only prevented by conditions so onerous and threatening that even the largest corporations here and abroad are unwilling to face the prospects (huge financial penalties and imprisonment for what Washington determines to be violations of "proper distribution," banning of ships and aircraft, mobilization of media campaigns, etc.). And while food shipments are indeed barred, the administration argues that there are "ample suppliers" elsewhere (at far higher cost), so that the direct violation of international law is not a violation.

As the issue was brought by the EU to the World Trade Organization, the United States withdrew from the proceedings on the ICJ model, effectively bringing the matter to a close.[10]

In short, the world that the United States has sought "to create in its image" through international institutions is one based on the principle of the rule of force. And the "American passion for free trade" entails that the U.S. government may violate trade agreements at will. No problem arises when communications, finance, and food supplies are taken over by foreign (mainly U.S.) corporations. Matters are different, however, when trade agreements and international law interfere with the projects of the powerful—again, in conformity with history's clear lessons.

We learn more by investigating the reasons for U.S. rejection of international law and trade agreements. In the Nicaragua case, State Department legal adviser Abraham Sofaer explained that when the United States accepted World Court jurisdiction in the 1940s, most members of the United Nations "were aligned with the United States and shared its views regarding world order." But now "a great many of these cannot be counted on to share our view of the original constitutional conception of the UN Charter," and "this same majority often opposes the United States on important international questions." It is therefore understandable that the United States should be far in the lead since the 1960s in vetoing UN resolutions on a wide range of issues, including international law, human rights, environmental protection, and so on, precisely contrary to the standard version repeated in the opening paragraph above. The United States advanced its lead another notch shortly after this account appeared, casting its seventy-first veto since 1967. When the question (Israeli settlements in Jerusalem) moved to the General Assembly, the United States and Israel stood alone in opposition, again a standard pattern.[11]

Drawing the natural conclusions from the unreliability of the world, Sofaer went on to explain that we must now "reserve to ourselves the power to determine whether the Court has jurisdiction over us in a particular case." The long-standing principle, now to be enforced in a world that is no longer sufficiently obedient, is that "the United States does not accept compulsory jurisdiction over any dispute involving matters essentially within the domestic jurisdiction of the United States, as determined by the United States." The "domestic matters" in question were the U.S. attack against Nicaragua.[12]

The basic operative principle was stated elegantly by the new Secretary of State, Madeleine Albright, when she lectured the UN Security Council about its unwillingness to go along with U.S. demands concerning Iraq: the U.S. will "behave, with others, multilaterally when we can and unilaterally as we must," recognizing no external constraints in an area deemed "vital to U.S. national interests"—as determined by the United States.[13] The UN is an appropriate forum when its members "can be counted on" to share Washington's views, but not when the majority "opposes the United States on important international questions." International law and democracy are fine things—but as judged by outcome, not process; like free trade.

The current U.S. stand in the WTO case thus breaks no new ground. Washington declared that the WTO "has no competence to proceed" on an issue of American national security; we are to understand that our existence is at stake in the strangulation of the Cuban economy. A WTO ruling against the United States in absentia would be of no significance or concern, a Clinton Administration spokesman added, because "we do not believe anything the WTO says or does can force the U.S. to change its laws." Recall that the great merit of the WTO telecommunications agreement was that this "new tool of foreign policy" forces other countries to change their laws and practices, in accord with our demands.

The principle is that the United States is exempt from WTO interference with its laws, just as it is free to violate international law at will; uniquely, though the privilege may be extended to client states as circumstances require. The fundamental principles of world order again resound, loud and clear.

The earlier GATT agreements had allowed for national security exceptions, and under them Washington had justified its embargo against Cuba as "measures taken in pursuit of essential U.S. security interests." The WTO agreement also permits a member to take "any action it considers necessary for the protection of its essential security interests," but only in relation to three designated issues: fissionable materials, traffic in armaments, and actions "taken in time of war or other emergency in international relations."[14] Perhaps not wishing to be officially on record with an utter absurdity, the Clinton administration did not formally invoke its "national security exemption," though it did make clear that the issue was "national security."

At the time of writing, the EU and the United States are trying to arrange a deal before April 14, when the WTO hearings are scheduled to begin. Meanwhile, the *Wall Street Journal* reports, Washington "says it won't cooperate with the WTO panels, arguing that the trade organization doesn't have jurisdiction over national security issues."[15]

Indecent Thoughts

Polite people are not supposed to remember the reaction when Kennedy tried to organize collective action against Cuba in 1961: Mexico could not go along, a diplomat explained, because "if we publicly declare that Cuba is a threat to our security, forty million Mexicans will die laughing."[16] Here we take a more sober view of threats to the national security.

There were also no reported deaths from laughter when administration spokesman Stuart Eizenstat, justifying Washington's rejection of the WTO agreements, argued that "Europe is challenging 'three decades of American Cuba policy that goes back to the Kennedy Administration,' and is aimed entirely at forcing a change of government in Havana."[17] A sober reaction is entirely in order on the assumption that the United States has every right to overthrow another government; in this case, by aggression, large-scale terror, and economic strangulation.

The assumption remains in place and apparently unchallenged, but Eizenstat's statement was criticized on narrower grounds by historian Arthur Schlesinger. Writing "as one involved in the Kennedy administration's Cuban policy," Schlesinger pointed out that Undersecretary of Commerce Eizenstat had misunderstood the policies of the Kennedy Administration. Its concern was Cuba's "troublemaking in the hemisphere" and "the Soviet connection." But these are now behind us, so the Clinton policies are an anachronism, though otherwise, it seems, unobjectionable.[18]

Schlesinger did not explain the meaning of the phrases "troublemaking in the hemisphere" and "the Soviet connection," but he has elsewhere, in secret. Reporting to the incoming president on the conclusions of a Latin American Mission in early 1961, Schlesinger spelled out the problem of Castro's "troublemaking": it is "the spread of the Castro idea of taking matters into one's own hands," a serious problem, he added shortly after, when "the distribution of land and other forms of national wealth greatly favors the propertied classes...[and] the poor and underprivileged, stimulated by the example of the Cuban revolution, are now demanding opportunities for a decent living." Schlesinger also explained the threat of the "Soviet connection": "Meanwhile, the Soviet Union hovers in the wings, flourishing large development loans and presenting itself as the model for achieving modernization in a single generation." The "Soviet connection" was perceived in a similar light far more broadly in Washington and London, from the origins of the cold war in 1917 into the 1960s, when the major documentary record currently ends.

Schlesinger also recommended to the incoming president "a certain amount of high-flown corn" about "the higher aims of culture and spirit," which "will thrill the audience south of the border, where metahistorical disquisitions are inordinately admired." Meanwhile we'll take care of serious matters. Just to show how much things change, Schlesinger also realistically criticized "the baleful influence of the International Monetary Fund," then pursuing the 1950s version of today's "Washington consensus" ("structural adjustment," "neoliberalism").[19]

With these (secret) explanations of Castro's "troublemaking in the hemisphere" and the "Soviet connection," we come a step closer to an understanding of the reality of the cold war. But that is another topic.

Similar troublemaking beyond the hemisphere has also been no slight problem, and continues to spread dangerous ideas among people who "are now demanding opportunities for a decent living." In late February 1996, while the United States was in an uproar over Cuba's downing of two planes of a Florida-based anti-Castro group that had regularly penetrated Cuban airspace, dropping leaflets in Havana calling on Cubans to revolt (also participating in the continuing terrorist attacks against Cuba, according to Cuban sources), the wire services were running different stories. AP reported that in South Africa "a cheering, singing crowd welcomed Cuban doctors" who had just arrived at the invitation of the Mandela government "to boost medical care in poor rural areas"; "Cuba has 57,000 doctors for its 11 million people, compared to 25,000 in South Africa for 40 million people." The 101 Cuban doctors included top medical specialists who, if they were South African, would "very likely be working in Cape Town or Johannesburg" at twice the salaries they will receive in the poor rural areas where they go. "Since the program of sending public health specialists overseas began in Algeria in 1963, Cuba has sent 51,820 doctors, dentists, nurses, and other medical doctors" to "the poorest third world nations," providing "medical aid totally free of charge" in most cases. A month after the South African welcome, Cuban medical experts were invited by Haiti to study a meningitis outbreak.[20]

A leading West German journal reported in 1988 that third world countries regard Cuba as "an international superpower" because of the teachers, construction workers, physicians, and others involved in "international service." In 1985, 16,000 Cubans worked in third world countries, more than twice the total of Peace Corps and AID specialists from the United States. By 1988, Cuba had "more physicians working abroad than any industrialized nation, and more than the UN's World Health Organization." Most of this aid is uncompensated, and Cuba's "international emissaries" are "men and women who live under conditions that most development aid workers would not accept," which is "the basis for their success." For Cubans, the report continues, "international service" is regarded as "a sign of political maturity" and taught in the schools as "the highest virtue." The warm reception by an ANC delegation in South Africa in 1996, and the crowds singing "Long Live Cuba," attest to the same phenomenon.[21]

On the side, we might ask how the United States would react to Libyan planes flying over New York and Washington, dropping leaflets calling on Americans to revolt, after years of terrorist attacks against U.S. targets at home and abroad. By garlanding them with flowers, perhaps? A hint was given by Barrie Dunsmore of ABC a few weeks before the downing of the two planes, citing Walter Porges, former ABC News vice-president for news practices. Porges reports that when an ABC news crew on a civilian plane attempted to take photographs of the U.S. Sixth Fleet in the Mediterranean, "it was told to move immediately or it would be shot down," which "would have been legal under provisions of International Law defining military air space." A small country under attack by a superpower is a different matter, however.[22]

A further look at history may be useful. The policy of overthrowing the government of Cuba does not go back to the Kennedy Administration, as Eizenstat asserted, but to its predecessor: the formal decision to overthrow Castro in favor of a regime "more devoted to the true interests of the Cuban people and more acceptable to the U.S." was taken in secret in March 1960, with the addendum that the operation must be carried out "in such a manner as to avoid any appearance of U.S. intervention," because of the expected reaction in Latin America and the need to ease the burden on doctrinal managers at home. At the time, the "Soviet connection" and "troublemaking in the hemisphere" were nil, apart from the Schlesingerian version. The Kennedy Administration also recognized that its efforts violated international law and the Charters of the UN and OAS, but such issues were dismissed without discussion, the declassified record reveals.[23]

Since Washington is the arbiter of the "true interests of the Cuban people," it was unnecessary for U.S. government planners to attend to the public opinion studies they received, reporting popular support for Castro and optimism about the future. For similar reasons, current information about these matters is of no account. The Clinton Administration is serving the true interests of the Cuban people by imposing misery and starvation, whatever studies of Cuban opinion may indicate. For example, polls reported in December 1994 by an affiliate of the Gallup organization found that half the population consider the embargo to be the "principal cause of Cuba's problems" while 3 percent found the political situation to be the "most serious problem facing Cuba today"; that 77 percent regard the U.S. as Cuba's "worst friend" (no one else reached 3 percent); that by two to one, the population feel that the revolution has registered more achievements than failures, the "principal failure" being "having depended on socialist countries like Russia which betrayed us"; and that half describe themselves as "revolutionary," another 20 percent "communist" or "socialist."[24]

Right or wrong, the conclusions about public attitudes are irrelevant, again a regular pattern, at home as well.

History buffs might recall that the policy actually dates back to the 1820s, when Washington's intention to take control of Cuba was blocked by the British deterrent. Cuba was regarded by Secretary of State John Quincy Adams as "an object of transcendent importance to the commercial and political interests of our Union," but he advised patience: over time, he predicted, Cuba would fall into U.S. hands by "the laws of political...gravitation," a "ripe fruit" for harvest. So it did, as power relations shifted enough for the United States to liberate the island (from its people) at the end of the century, turning it into a U.S. plantation and haven for crime syndicates and tourists.

The historical depth of the commitment to rule Cuba may help account for the element of hysteria so apparent in the execution of the enterprise; for example, the "almost savage" atmosphere of the first cabinet meeting after the failed Bay of Pigs invasion described by Chester Bowles, the "almost frantic reaction for an action program," a mood reflected in President

Kennedy's public statements about how failure to act would leave us "about to be swept away with the debris of history." Clinton's initiatives, public and indirect, reveal a similar streak of vindictive fanaticism, as in the threats and prosecutions that ensured that "the number of companies granted U.S. licenses to sell [medicines] to Cuba has fallen to less than 4 percent" of the levels prior to the Cuban Democracy Act (CDA) of October 1992, while "only a few of the world's medical companies have attempted to brave U.S. regulations" and penalties, a review in Britain's leading medical journal reports.[25]

Considerations such as these carry us from the abstract plane of international law and solemn agreements to the realities of human life. Lawyers may debate whether the ban on food and (effectively) medicine violates international agreements stating that "food must not be used as an instrument for political and economic pressure" (Rome Declaration, 1996) and other declared principles and commitments. But the victims have to live with the fact that the CDA has "resulted in a serious reduction in the trade of legitimate medical supplies and food donations, to the detriment of the Cuban people" (Cameron). A recently released study of the American Association for World Health (AAWH) concludes that the embargo has caused serious nutritional deficits, deterioration in the supply of safe drinking water, and sharp decline in availability of medicines and medical information, leading to a low birth rate, epidemics of neurological and other diseases with tens of thousands of victims, and other severe health consequences. "Health and nutrition standards have been devastated by the recent tightening of the 37-year-old U.S. embargo, which includes food imports," Victoria Brittain writes in the British press, reporting the year-long AAWH study by U.S. specialists, which found "hospitalised children lying in agony as essential drugs are denied them" and doctors compelled "to work with medical equipment at less than half efficiency because they have no spare parts." Similar conclusions are drawn in other current studies in professional journals.[26]

These are the real crimes, far more than the casual and reflexive violation of legal instruments that are used as weapons against official enemies, with the cynicism that only the truly powerful can display.

In fairness, it should be added that the suffering caused by the embargo is sometimes reported here as well. A lead story in the *New York Times* business section is headlined "Exploding Cuban Cigar Prices: Now Embargo Really Hurts as Big Smokes Grow Scarcer." The story reports the tribulations of business executives at "a plush smoking room" in Manhattan, who lament "that it's really tough to get a Cuban cigar in the States these days" except at "prices that catch in the throats of the most devoted smokers."[27]

While the Clinton Administration, exploiting the privilege of the powerful, attributes the grim consequences of economic warfare without parallel in current history to the policies of the regime from which it promises to "liberate" the suffering Cuban people, a more plausible conclusion is more nearly the reverse: the "American economic strangulation of Cuba" has been designed, maintained, and in the post-cold-war era intensified, for the reasons implicit in Arthur Schlesinger's report to incoming President Kennedy. Much as Kennedy's Latin American Mission feared, the successes of programs to improve health and living standards had been helping to spread "the Castro idea of taking matters into one's own hands," stimulating "the poor and underprivileged" in the region with the worst inequality in the world to "demand opportunities for a decent living," and with dangerous effects beyond as well. There is a substantial and compelling documentary record, accompanied by consistent action based on quite rational motives, which lends no slight credibility to this assessment. To evaluate the claim that the policies flow from concern for human rights and democracy, the briefest look at the record is more than sufficient, at least for those who even pretend to be serious.

It is improper, however, to have any thoughts or recollections about such matters as we celebrate the triumph of "American values." Nor are we supposed to remember that Clinton, inspired by the same passion for free trade, "pressured Mexico into an agreement that will end the shipment of low-price tomatoes to the United States," a gift to Florida growers that costs Mexico about $800 million annually, and that violates NAFTA as well as the WTO agreements (though only "in spirit," because it was a sheer power play and did not require an official tariff). The administration explained the decision forthrightly: Mexican tomatoes are cheaper, and consumers here prefer them. The free market is working, but with the wrong outcome. Or perhaps tomatoes too are a threat to national security.[28]

To be sure, tomatoes and telecommunications are in very different leagues. Any favors Clinton might owe to Florida growers are dwarfed by the requirements of the telecommunications industry, even apart from what Thomas Ferguson describes as "the best-kept secret of the 1996 election": that "more than any other single bloc, it was the telecommunications sector that rescued Bill Clinton," who received major campaign contributions from "this staggeringly profitable sector." The Telecommunications Act of 1996 and the WTO agreement are, in a sense, thank-you notes, though it is unlikely that the outcome would have been very different if a different mix of largesse had been chosen by the business world, suffering at the time from what *Business Week* had just called "spectacular" profits in yet another "Surprise Party for Corporate America."[29]

Prominent among the truths that are not to be recalled are the ones briefly mentioned earlier: the actual record of "Reaganesque rugged individualism" and the "free market gospel" that was preached (to the poor and defenseless) while protectionism reached unprecedented heights and the administration poured public funds into high-tech industry with unusual abandon. Here we begin to reach the heart of the matter. The reasons for skepticism about the "passion" that have just been reviewed are valid enough, but they are a footnote to the real story: how U.S. corporations came to be so well placed to take over international markets, inspiring the current celebration of "American values."

But that, again, is a larger tale, one that tells us a lot about the contemporary world: its social and economic realities, and the grip of ideology and doctrine, including those doctrines crafted to induce hopelessness, resignation, and despair.

First published in Z, March 1997.

Notes

1. David Sanger, *NYT*, February 17, 1997; Youssef Ibrahim, *NYT*, December 13, 1996; Harvey Cox, *World Policy Review*, Spring 1997; Martin Nolan, *Boston Globe*, March 5, 1997; John Buell, *Progressive*, March 1997.

2. Shafiqul Islam, *Foreign Affairs, America and the World*, 1989-90.

3. Patrick Low, *Trading Free* (Twentieth Century Fund, 1993).

4. *Observer* (London), January 19, January 12, 1997; also Noam Chomsky, *Powers and Prospects* (South End, 1996), 18;. *Independent*, November 24, 25, 1996, *Guardian Weekly*, January 5, 1997 *Financial Times*, January 17, 1997.

5. Gary Silverman and Shada Islam, *Far Eastern Economic Review*, February 27, 1997.

6. Reuters, February 1, 1996, cited in Andrew Grove, *Only the Paranoid Survive* (Doubleday, 1996), 201, 172-3. On the prospects, see Robert McChesney, *Corporate Media and the Threat to Democracy* (Open Media Pamphlet Series/Seven Stories Press, 1997); Edward Herman and Robert McChesney, *The Global Media* (Cassell, 1997).

7. *Jornal do Brasil*, March 10, 19, 1997; *Revista Atencao*, March 1997, reprinted in *Sem Terra*, February 1997; Carlos Tautz, *Latinamerica Press*, March 13, 1997.

8. Deborah Hargreaves, *Financial Times* (London), February 2, 1996.

9. Editorial, *NYT*, February 17, 1997; Peter Morici, *Current History*, February 1997.

10. Editorial, *NYT*, February 17, 1997; *NYT*, November 13, 1996; Wayne Smith, *In These Times*, December 9, 1996; Anthony Kirkpatrick, *Lancet* 358, no.9040, November 30, 1996, reprinted in *Cuba Update*, Winter 1997; David Sanger, *NYT*, February 21, 1997.

11. Ian Williams, *Middle East International*, March 21, 1997. On the fanciful standard rendition of the UN record, see Noam Chomsky, *Deterring Democracy* (Verso 1991), Chapter 6; *Letters from Lexington* (Common Courage, 1993), Chapters 8, 9.

12. Abraham Sofaer, *The United States and the World Court*, U.S. Dept. of State, Bureau of Public Affairs, Current Policy Series, no. 769 ,December 1985.

13. Jules Kagian, *Middle East International*, October 21, 1994.

14. Frances Williams and Nancy Dunne, *Financial Times*, November 21, 1996.

15. *Wall Street Journal*, March 25, 1997.

16. Ruth Leacock, *Requiem for Revolution* (Kent State, 1990), 33.

17. David Sanger, *NYT*, February 21, 1997.

18. Arthur Schlesinger, letter, *NYT*, February 26, 1997.

19. *Foreign Relations of the United States*, 1961-63, vol. XII, *American Republics*, 13f., 33, 9. (Government Printing Office, Washington, DC 1997.

20. Tim Weiner and Miyera Navarro, *NYT*, February 26, 1997, reporting also that U.S. intelligence said at least one of the planes, perhaps all three, had violated Cuban airspace and had received warnings from air traffic control in Havana. On recent terrorist attacks, see *Cuba Update*, March/April 1996. Angus Shaw, AP, February 27; Donna Bryson, AP, February 20; Lionel Martin, Reuters, March 26, 1996 (service of *San Jose Mercury News*). *Boston Globe*, March 24, 1996.

21. Michael Stuehrenberg, *Die Zeit*; *World Press Review*, December 1988.

22. Barrie Dunsmore, "Live from the Battlefield," discussion paper, January 8, 1996.

23. Piero Gleijeses, "Ships in the Night: The CIA, the White House and the Bay of Pigs," *Journal of Latin American Studies* 27, no. 1, February 1995, 1-42; Jules Benjamin, *The United States and the Origins of the Cuban Revolution* (Princeton University Press, 1990).

24. *Miami Herald*, Spanish edition, December 18, 1994; Maria Lopez Vigil, *Envío* (Jesuit University of Central America, Managua), June 1995.

25. Kirkpatrick, *op. cit.* Joanna Cameron, "The Cuban Democracy Act of 1992: The International Complications," *Fletcher Forum* (Winter/Spring

1996). See Noam Chomsky, *Year 501* (South End, 1993), Chapter. 6, for background and sources.

26. Cameron, *"Cuban Democracy Act"*; American Association for World Health, *Denial of Food and Medicine: the Impact of the U.S. Embargo on Health and Nutrition in Cuba*, March 1997; Victoria Brittain, *Guardian Weekly*, March 16, 1997.

27. *NYT*, April 17, 1996.

28. David Sanger, *NYT*, October 12, 1996. A year later, the Clinton Administration imposed high tariffs on Japanese supercomputers. See Chapter VII, below.

29. Thomas Ferguson, *Mother Jones*, November/December 1996; *Business Week*, August 12, 1996.

IV

Market Democracy in a Neoliberal Order

Doctrines and Reality

IV

**Excerpted from the annual Davie Memorial Lecture delivered at the
University of Cape Town, South Africa, May 1997.**

I have been asked to speak on some aspect of academic or
human freedom, an invitation that offers many choices. I will keep
to some simple ones.

Freedom without opportunity is a devil's gift, and the
refusal to provide such opportunities is criminal. The fate of the
more vulnerable offers a sharper measure of the distance from here
to something that might be called "civilization." While I am speaking, 1,000 children will die from easily preventable disease, and
almost twice that many women will die or suffer serious disabil-
ity in pregnancy or childbirth for lack of simple remedies and care.[1]
UNICEF estimates that to overcome such tragedies, and to ensure
universal access to basic social services, would require a quarter
of the annual military expenditures of the "developing countries,"
about 10 percent of U.S. military spending. It is against the background of such realities as these that any serious discussion of
human freedom should proceed.

It is widely held that the cure for such profound social maladies is within reach. This hope is not without foundation. The past few years have seen the fall of brutal tyrannies, the growth of scientific understanding that offers great promise, and many other reasons to look forward to a brighter future. The discourse of the privileged is marked by confidence and triumphalism: the way forward is known, and there is no other. The basic theme, articulated with force and clarity, is that "America's victory in the cold war was a victory for a set of political and economic princi-ples: democracy and the free market." These principles are "the wave of the future—a future for which America is both the gate-keeper and the model." I am quoting the chief political commen-tator of the *New York Times,* but the picture is conventional, widely repeated throughout much of the world, and accepted as gener-ally accurate even by critics. It was also enunciated as the "Clin-ton Doctrine," which declared that our new mission is to "consolidate the victory of democracy and open markets" that had just been won.

There remains a range of disagreement: at one extreme "Wilsonian idealists" urge continued dedication to the traditional mission of benevolence, and at the other, "realists" counter that we may lack the means to conduct these crusades of "global melior-ism," and should not neglect our own interests in the service of others. Within this range lies the path to a better world.[2]

Reality seems to me rather different. The current spectrum of public policy debate has as little relevance to policy as its numer-ous antecedents: neither the United States nor any other power has been guided by "global meliorism." Democracy is under attack worldwide, including the leading industrial countries; at least, democracy in a meaningful sense of the term, involving opportu-nities for people to manage their own collective and individual affairs. Something similar is true of markets. The assaults on democ-racy and markets are furthermore related. Their roots lie in the power of corporate entities that are increasingly interlinked and reliant on powerful states, and largely unaccountable to the pub-lic. Their immense power is growing as a result of social policy that is globalizing the structural model of the third world, with sectors of enormous wealth and privilege alongside an increase in "the proportion of those who will labor under all the hardships of life, and secretly sigh for a more equal distribution of its blessings," as the leading framer of American democracy, James Madison, predicted 200 years ago.[3] These policy choices are most evident in the Anglo-American societies, but extend worldwide. They cannot be attributed to what "the free market has decided, in its infinite but mysterious wisdom,"[4] "the implacable sweep of 'the market revolution,'" "Reaganesque rugged individualism," or a "new orthodoxy" that "gives the market full sway." On the contrary, state intervention plays a decisive role, as in the past, and the basic outlines of policy are hardly novel. Current versions reflect "capital's clear subjugation of labor" for more than fifteen years, in the words of the business press,[5] which often accurately reports the perceptions of a highly class-conscious business community, dedicated to class war.

If these perceptions are valid, then the path to a world that is more just and more free lies well outside the range set forth by privilege and power. I cannot hope to establish such conclusions here, but only to suggest that they are credible enough to consider with care. And to suggest further that prevailing doctrines could hardly survive were it not for their contribution to "regimenting the public mind every bit as much as an army regiments the bodies of its soldiers," to quote again from Edward Bernays while presenting to the business world the lessons that had been learned from wartime propaganda (see page 53f.).

Quite strikingly, in both of the world's leading democracies there was a growing awareness of the need to "apply the lessons" of the highly successful propaganda systems of World War I "to the organization of political warfare," as the chairman of the British Conservative party put the matter seventy years ago. Wilsonian liberals in the United States, including public intellectuals and prominent figures in the developing profession of political science, drew the same conclusions in the same years. In another corner of Western civilization, Adolf Hitler vowed that next time Germany would not be defeated in the propaganda war, and he also devised his own ways to apply the lessons of Anglo-American propaganda to political warfare at home.[6]

Meanwhile the business world warned of "the hazard facing industrialists" in "the newly realized political power of the masses," and the need to wage and win "the everlasting battle for the minds of men" and "indoctrinate citizens with the capitalist story" until "they are able to play back the story with remarkable fidelity"; and so on, in an impressive flow, accompanied by even more impressive efforts.[7]

To discover the true meaning of the "political and economic principles" that are declared to be "the wave of the future," it is of course necessary to go beyond rhetorical flourishes and public pronouncements and to investigate actual practice and the internal documentary record. Close examination of particular cases is the most rewarding path, but these must be chosen carefully to give a fair picture. There are some natural guidelines. One reasonable approach is to take the examples chosen by the proponents of the doctrines themselves, as their strongest case. Another is to investigate the record where influence is greatest and interference least, so that we see the operative principles in their purest form. If we want to determine what the Kremlin meant by "democracy" and "human rights," we will pay little heed to *Pravda*'s solemn denunciations of racism in the United States or state terror in its client regimes, even less to protestation of noble motives. Far more instructive is the state of affairs in the "people's democracies" of Eastern Europe. The point is elementary, and applies to the self-designated "gatekeeper and model" as well. Latin America is the obvious testing ground, particularly the Central America-Caribbean region. Here Washington has faced few external challenges for almost a century, so the guiding principles of policy, and of today's neoliberal "Washington consensus," are revealed most clearly when we examine the state of the region, and how that came about.

It is of some interest that the exercise is rarely undertaken, and if proposed, castigated as extremist or worse. I leave it as an "exercise for the reader," merely noting that the record teaches useful lessons about the political and economic principles that are to be "the wave of the future."

Washington's "crusade for democracy," as it is called, was waged with particular fervor during the Reagan years, with Latin America serving as the chosen terrain. The results are commonly offered as a prime illustration of how the United States became "the inspiration for the triumph of democracy in our time," to quote the editors of a leading intellectual journal of American liberalism.[8] The most recent scholarly study of democracy describes "the revival of democracy in Latin America" as "impressive" but not unproblematic; the "barriers to implementation" remain "formidable," but can be perhaps be overcome through closer integration with the United States. The author, Sanford Lakoff, singles out the "historic North American Free Trade Agreement (NAFTA)" as a potential instrument of democratization. In the region of traditional U.S. influence, he writes, the countries are moving toward democracy, having "survived military intervention" and "vicious civil war."[9]

Let us begin by looking more closely at these recent cases, the natural ones given overwhelming U.S. influence, and the ones regularly selected to illustrate the achievements and promise of "America's mission."

The primary "barriers to implementation" of democracy, Lakoff suggests, are efforts to protect "domestic markets"—that is, to prevent foreign (mainly U.S.) corporations from gaining even greater control over the society. We are to understand, then, that democracy is enhanced as significant decision making shifts even more into the hands of unaccountable private tyrannies, mostly foreign-based. Meanwhile the public arena is to shrink still further as the state is "minimized" in accordance with the neoliberal political and economic principles that have emerged triumphant. A study of the World Bank points out that the new orthodoxy represents "a dramatic shift away from a pluralist, participatory ideal of politics and towards an authoritarian and technocratic ideal," one that is very much in accord with leading elements of twentieth century liberal and progressive thought, and in another variant, the Leninist model; the two are more similar than often recognized.[10]

Thinking through the background, we gain some useful insight into the concepts of democracy and markets, in the operative sense.

Lakoff does not look into the "revival of democracy" in Latin America, but he does cite a scholarly source that includes a contribution on Washington's crusade in the 1980s. The author is Thomas Carothers, who combines scholarship with an "insider's perspective," having worked on "democracy enhancement" programs in Reagan's State Department.[11] Carothers regards Washington's "impulse to promote democracy" as "sincere," but largely a failure. Furthermore, the failure was systematic: where Washington's influence was least, in South America, there was real progress toward democracy, which the Reagan Administration generally opposed, later taking credit for it when the process proved irresistible. Where Washington's influence was greatest, progress was least, and where it occurred, the U.S. role was marginal or negative. His general conclusion is that the U.S. sought to maintain "the basic order of...quite undemocratic societies" and to avoid "populist-based change," "inevitably [seeking] only limited, top-down forms of democratic change that did not risk upsetting the traditional structures of power with which the United States has long been allied."

The last clause requires a gloss. The term *United States* is conventionally used to refer to structures of power within the United States; the "national interest" is the interest of these groups, which correlates only weakly with interests of the general population. So the conclusion is that Washington sought top-down forms of democracy that did not upset traditional structures of power with which the structures of power in the United States have long been allied. Not a very surprising fact, or much of a historical novelty.

Within the United States itself, "top-down democracy" is firmly rooted in the Constitutional system.[12] One may argue, as some historians do, that these principles lost their force as the national territory was conquered and settled. Whatever one's assessment of those years, by the late nineteenth century the founding doctrines took on a new and much more oppressive form. When James Madison spoke of "rights of persons," he meant *persons.* But the growth of the industrial economy, and the rise of corporate forms of economic enterprise, led to a completely new meaning of the term. In a current official document, "'*Person*' is broadly defined to include any individual, branch, partnership, associated group, association, estate, trust, corporation or other organization (whether or not organized under the laws of any State), or any government entity,"[13] a concept that would have shocked Madison and others with intellectual roots in the Enlightenment and classical liberalism.

These radical changes in the conception of human rights and democracy were introduced primarily not by legislation but by judicial decisions and intellectual commentary. Corporations, which previously had been considered artificial entities with no rights, were accorded all the rights of persons, and far more, since they are "immortal persons," and "persons" of extraordinary wealth and power. Furthermore, they were no longer bound to the specific purposes designated by State charter but could act as they chose, with few constraints.[14]

Conservative legal scholars bitterly opposed these innovations, recognizing that they undermine the traditional idea that rights inhere in individuals, and undermine market principles as well. But the new forms of authoritarian rule were institutionalized, and along with them the legitimation of wage labor, which was considered hardly better than slavery in mainstream American thought through much of the nineteenth century, not only by the rising labor movement but also by such figures as Abraham Lincoln, the Republican party, and the establishment media.[15]

These are topics with enormous implications for understanding the nature of market democracy. Again, I can only mention them here. The material and ideological outcome helps explain the understanding that "democracy" abroad must reflect the model sought at home: top-down forms of control, with the public kept to a spectator role, not participating in the arena of decision making, which must exclude these "ignorant and meddlesome outsiders," according to the mainstream of modern democratic theory. But the general ideas are standard and have solid roots in the tradition, radically modified, however, in the new era of "collectivist legal entities."

Returning to the "victory of democracy" under U.S. guidance, neither Lakoff nor Carothers asks how Washington maintained the traditional power structure of highly undemocratic societies. Their topic is not the terrorist wars that left tens of thousands of tortured and mutilated corpses, millions of refugees, and devastation perhaps beyond recovery—in large measure wars against the Church, which became an enemy when it adopted "the preferential option for the poor," trying to help suffering people to attain some measure of justice and democratic rights. It is more than symbolic that the terrible decade of the 1980s opened with the murder of an archbishop who had become "a voice for the voiceless," and closed with the assassination of six leading Jesuit intellectuals who had chosen the same path, in each case by terrorist forces armed and trained by the victors of the "crusade for democracy." One should take careful note of the fact that the leading Central American dissident intellectuals were doubly assassinated: both murdered and silenced. Their words, indeed their very existence, are scarcely known in the United States, unlike dissidents in enemy states, who are greatly honored and admired.

Such matters do not enter history as recounted by the victors. In Lakoff's study, which is not untypical in this regard, what survives are references to "military intervention" and "civil wars," with no external factor identified. These matters will not so quickly be put aside, however, by those who seek a better grasp of the principles that are to shape the future, if the structures of power have their way.

Particularly revealing is Lakoff's description of Nicaragua, again standard: "A civil war was ended following a democratic election, and a difficult effort is underway to create a more prosperous and self-governing society." In the real world, the superpower attacking Nicaragua escalated its assault *after* the country's first democratic election. The election of 1984 was closely monitored and recognized as legitimate by the professional association of Latin American scholars (LASA), Irish and British parliamentary delegations, and others, including a hostile Dutch government delegation that was remarkably supportive of Reaganite atrocities. The leading figure of Central American democracy, José Figueres of Costa Rica, also a critical observer, nevertheless regarded the elections as legitimate in this "invaded country," calling on Washington to allow the Sandinistas "to finish what they started in peace; they deserve it." The United States strongly opposed the holding of the elections and sought to undermine them, concerned that democratic elections might interfere with its terrorist war. But that concern was put to rest by the good behavior of the doctrinal system, which barred the reports with remarkable efficiency, reflexively adopting the state propaganda line that the elections were meaningless fraud.[16]

Overlooked as well is the fact that as the next election approached on schedule,[17] Washington left no doubt that unless the results came out the right way, Nicaraguans would continue to endure the illegal economic warfare and "unlawful use of force" that the World Court had condemned and ordered terminated, of course in vain. This time the outcome was acceptable, and hailed in the United States with an outburst of exuberance that is highly informative.[18]

At the outer limits of critical independence, columnist Anthony Lewis of the *New York Times* was overcome with admiration for Washington's "experiment in peace and democracy," which showed that "we live in a romantic age." The experimental methods were no secret. Thus *Time* magazine, joining in the celebration as "democracy burst forth" in Nicaragua, outlined them frankly: to "wreck the economy and prosecute a long and deadly proxy war until the exhausted natives overthrow the unwanted government themselves," with a cost to us that is "minimal," leaving the victim "with wrecked bridges, sabotaged power stations, and ruined farms," and providing Washington's candidate with "a winning issue," ending the "impoverishment of the people of Nicaragua," not to speak of the continuing terror, better left unmentioned. To be sure, the cost to *them* was hardly "minimal": Carothers notes that the toll "in per capita terms was significantly higher than the number of U.S. persons killed in the U.S. Civil War and all the wars of the twentieth century *combined*."[19] The outcome was a "Victory for U.S. Fair Play," a headline in the *New York Times* exulted, leaving Americans "United in Joy," in the style of Albania and North Korea.

The methods of this "romantic age," and the reaction to them in enlightened circles, tell us more about the democratic principles that have emerged victorious. They also shed some light on why it is such a "difficult effort" to "create a more prosperous and self-governing society" in Nicaragua. It is true that the effort is now underway, and is meeting with some success for a privileged minority, while most of the population faces social and economic disaster, all in the familiar pattern of Western dependencies.[20] Note that it is this example that led the *New Republic* editors to laud themselves as "the inspiration for the triumph of democracy in our time," joining the enthusiastic chorus.

We learn more about the victorious principles by recalling that these same representative figures of liberal intellectual life had urged that Washington's wars must be waged mercilessly, with military support for "Latin-style fascists...regardless of how many are murdered," because "there are higher American priorities than Salvadoran human rights." Elaborating, *New Republic* editor Michael Kinsley, who represented the left in mainstream commentary and television debate, cautioned against unthinking criticism of Washington's official policy of attacking undefended civilian targets. Such international terrorist operations cause "vast civilian suffering," he acknowledged, but they may be "perfectly legitimate" if "cost-benefit analysis" shows that "the amount of blood and misery that will be poured in" yields "democracy," as the world rulers define it. Enlightened opinion insists that terror is not a value in itself, but must meet the pragmatic criterion. Kinsley later observed that the desired ends had been achieved: "Impoverishing the people of Nicaragua was precisely the point of the contra war and the parallel policy of economic embargo and veto of international development loans," which "wreck[ed] the economy" and "creat[ed] the economic disaster [that] was probably the victorious opposition's best election issue." He then joined in welcoming the "triumph of democracy" in the "free election" of 1990.[21]

Client states enjoy similar privileges. Thus, commenting on yet another of Israel's attacks on Lebanon, foreign editor H.D.S. Greenway of the *Boston Globe*, who had graphically reported the first major invasion fifteen years earlier, commented that "if shelling Lebanese villages, even at the cost of lives, and driving civilian refugees north would secure Israel's border, weaken Hezbollah, and promote peace, I would say go to it, as would many Arabs and Israelis. But history has not been kind to Israeli adventures in Lebanon. They have solved very little and have almost always caused more problems." By the pragmatic criterion, then, the murder of many civilians, expulsion of hundreds of thousand of refugees, and devastation of southern Lebanon is a dubious proposition.[22]

Bear in mind that I am keeping to the dissident sector of tolerable opinion, what is called "the left," a fact that tells us more about the victorious principles and the intellectual culture within which they find their place.

Also revealing was the reaction to periodic Reagan Administration allegations of Nicaraguan plans to obtain jet interceptors from the Soviet Union (the United States having coerced its allies into refusing to sell them). Hawks demanded that Nicaragua be bombed at once. Doves countered that the charges must first be verified, but if they were, the United States would have to bomb Nicaragua. Sane observers understood why Nicaragua might want

jet interceptors: to protect its territory from CIA overflights that
were supplying the U.S. proxy forces and providing them with up-
to-the-minute information so that they could follow the directive
to attack undefended "soft targets." The tacit assumption is that
no country has a right to defend civilians from U.S. attack, a doctrine that reigned virtually unchallenged in the mainstream.

The pretext for Washington's terrorist wars was self-
defense, the standard official justification for just about any monstrous act, even the Nazi Holocaust. Indeed Ronald Reagan,
finding "that the policies and actions of the government of
Nicaragua constitute an unusual and extraordinary threat to the
national security and foreign policy of the United States," declared
"a national emergency to deal with that threat," arousing no
ridicule.[23] By similar logic, the USSR had every right to attack
Denmark, a far greater threat to its security, and surely Poland and
Hungary when they took steps toward independence. The fact
that such pleas can regularly be put forth is again an interesting
comment on the intellectual culture of the victors, and another
indication of what lies ahead.

Let us move on to NAFTA, the "historic" agreement that
may help to advance U.S.-style democracy in Mexico, Lakoff suggests. A closer look is again informative. The NAFTA agreement
was rammed through Congress over strenuous popular opposition
but with overwhelming support from the business world and the
media, which were full of joyous promises of benefits for all concerned, also confidently predicted by the U.S. International Trade
Commission and leading economists equipped with the most up-
to-date models (which had just failed miserably to predict the deleterious consequences of the U.S.-Canada Free Trade Agreement,
but were somehow going to work in this case). Completely suppressed was the careful analysis by the Office of Technology
Assessment (the research bureau of Congress), which concluded
that the planned version of NAFTA would harm most of the population of North America, proposing modifications that could ren-
der the agreement beneficial beyond small circles of investment

and finance. Still more instructive was the suppression of the official position of the U.S. labor movement, presented in a similar analysis. Meanwhile labor was bitterly condemned for its "backward, unenlightened" perspective and "crude threatening tactics," motivated by "fear of change and fear of foreigners"; I am again sampling only from the far left of the spectrum, in this case, Anthony Lewis. The charges were demonstrably false, but they were the only word that reached the public in this inspiring exercise of democracy. Further details are most illuminating, and reviewed in the dissident literature at the time and since, but kept from the public eye, and unlikely to enter approved history.[24]

By now, the tales about the wonders of NAFTA have quietly been shelved, as the facts have been coming in. One hears no more about the hundreds of thousands of new jobs and other great benefits in store for the people of the three countries. These good tidings have been replaced by the "distinctly benign economic viewpoint"—the "experts' view"—that NAFTA had *no* significant effects. The *Wall Street Journal* reports that "administration officials feel frustrated by their inability to convince voters that the threat doesn't hurt them" and that job loss is "much less than predicted by Ross Perot," who was allowed into mainstream discussion (unlike the OTA, the Labor movement, economists who strayed from the Party Line, and of course dissident analysts) because his claims were sometimes extreme and easily ridiculed. Quoting the sad observation of an administration official, the *Journal* reports further that "'It's hard to fight the critics' by telling the truth—that the trade pact 'hasn't really done anything.'" Forgotten is what "the truth" was going to be when the impressive exercise in democracy was roaring full steam ahead.[25]

While the experts have downgraded NAFTA to "no significant effects," dispatching the earlier "experts' view" to the memory hole, a less than "distinctly benign economic viewpoint" comes into focus if the "national interest" is widened in scope to include the general population. Testifying before the Senate Banking Committee in February 1997, Federal Reserve Board Chair Alan

Greenspan was highly optimistic about "sustainable economic expansion" thanks to "atypical restraint on compensation increases [which] appears to be mainly the consequence of greater worker insecurity"—an obvious desideratum for a just society. The February 1997 Economic Report of the President, taking pride in the administration's achievements, refers more obliquely to "changes in labor market institutions and practices" as a factor in the "significant wage restraint" that bolsters the health of the economy.

One reason for these benign changes is spelled out in a study commissioned by the NAFTA Labor Secretariat "on the effects of the sudden closing of the plant on the principle of freedom of association and the right of workers to organize in the three countries." The study was carried out under NAFTA rules in response to a complaint by telecommunications workers on illegal labor practices by Sprint. The complaint was upheld by the U.S. National Labor Relations Board, which ordered trivial penalties after years of delay, standard procedure. The NAFTA study, by Cornell University Labor economist Kate Bronfenbrenner, was authorized for release by Canada and Mexico, but delayed by the Clinton Administration. It reveals a significant impact of NAFTA on strike-breaking. About half of union organizing efforts are disrupted by employer threats to transfer production abroad; for example, by placing signs reading "Mexico Transfer Job" in front of a plant where there is an organizing drive. The threats are not idle: when such organizing drives nevertheless succeed, employers close the plant in whole or in part at triple the pre-NAFTA rate (about 15 percent of the time). Plant-closing threats are almost twice as high in more mobile industries (e.g., manufacturing vs. construction).

These and other practices reported in the study are illegal, but that is a technicality, on a par with violations of international law and trade agreements when outcomes are unacceptable. The Reagan Administration had made it clear to the business world that their illegal anti-union activities would not be hampered by the criminal state, and successors have kept to this stand. There has been a substantial effect on destruction of unions—or in more polite words, "changes in labor market institutions and practices" that contribute to "significant wage restraint" within an economic model offered with great pride to a backward world that has not yet grasped the victorious principles that are to lead the way to freedom and justice.[26]

What was stressed outside the mainstream about the goals of NAFTA is also now quietly conceded: the real goal was to "lock Mexico in" to the "reforms" that had made it an "economic miracle," in the technical sense of this term: a "miracle" for U.S. investors and the Mexican rich, while the population sank into misery. The Clinton Administration "forgot that the underlying purpose of NAFTA was not to promote trade but to cement Mexico's economic reforms," *Newsweek* correspondent Marc Levinson loftily declares, failing only to add that the contrary was loudly proclaimed to ensure the passage of NAFTA while critics who pointed out this "underlying purpose" were largely excluded from the free market of ideas by its owners.

Perhaps someday the likely reasons will be conceded too. "Locking Mexico in" to these reforms, it was hoped, would deflect the danger detected by a Latin America Strategy Development Workshop in Washington in September 1990. It concluded that relations with the brutal Mexican dictatorship were fine, though there was a potential problem: "a 'democracy opening' in Mexico could test the special relationship by bringing into office a government more interested in challenging the U.S. on economic and nationalist grounds"—no longer a serious problem now that Mexico is "locked into the reforms" by treaty. The U.S. has the power to disregard treaty obligations at will; not Mexico.[27]

In brief, the threat is democracy, at home and abroad, as the chosen example again illustrates. Democracy is permissible, even welcome, but again, as judged by outcome, not process. NAFTA was considered to be an effective device to diminish the threat of democracy. It was implemented at home by effective subversion of the democratic process, and in Mexico by force, over substantial but vain public protest.[28] The results are now presented as a hopeful instrument to bring American-style democracy to benighted Mexicans. A cynical observer aware of the facts might agree.

Once again, the chosen illustrations of the triumph of democracy are natural ones, and are interesting and revealing as well, though not quite in the intended manner.

The announcement of the Clinton Doctrine was accompanied by a prize example to illustrate the victorious principles: the administration's achievement in Haiti. Since this is again offered as the strongest case, it is appropriate to look at it.

True, Haiti's elected president was allowed to return, but only after the popular organizations had been subjected to three years of terror by forces that retained close connections to Washington throughout; the Clinton Administration still refuses to turn over to Haiti 160,000 pages of documents on state terror seized by U.S. military forces—"to avoid embarrassing revelations" about U.S. government involvement with the coup regime, according to Human Rights Watch.[29] It was also necessary to put President Aristide through "a crash course in democracy and capitalism," as his leading supporter in Washington described the process of civilizing the troublesome priest.

The device is not unknown elsewhere, as an unwelcome transition to formal democracy is contemplated.

As a condition on his return, Aristide was compelled to accept an economic program that directs the policies of the Haitian government to the needs of "Civil Society, especially the private sector, both national and foreign": U.S. investors are designated to be the core of Haitian civil society, along with wealthy Haitians who backed the military coup, but not the Haitian peasants and slum dwellers who organized a civil society so lively and vibrant that they were even able to elect their own president against overwhelming odds, eliciting instant U.S. hostility and efforts to subvert Haiti's first democratic regime.[30]

The unacceptable acts of the "ignorant and meddlesome outsiders" in Haiti were reversed by violence, with direct U.S. complicity, not only through contacts with the state terrorists in charge. The Organization of American States declared an embargo. The Bush and Clinton Administrations undermined it from the start by exempting U.S. firms, and also by secretly authorizing the Texaco Oil Company to supply the coup regime and its wealthy supporters in violation of the official sanctions, a crucial fact that was prominently revealed the day before U.S. troops landed to "restore democracy"[31] but has yet to reach the public, and is another unlikely candidate for the historical record.

Now democracy has been restored. The new government has been forced to abandon the democratic and reformist programs that scandalized Washington, and to follow the policies of Washington's candidate in the 1990 election, in which he received 14 percent of the vote.

The background of this triumph provides no little insight into the "political and economic principles" that are to lead us to a glorious future. Haiti was one of the world's richest colonial prizes (along with Bengal) and the source of a good part of France's wealth. It has been largely under U.S. control and tutelage since Wilson's Marines invaded eighty years ago. By now the country is such a catastrophe that it may scarcely be habitable in the not-too-distant future. In 1981 a USAID-World Bank development strategy was initiated, based on assembly plants and agroexport, shifting land from food for local consumption. USAID forecast "a historic change toward deeper market interdependence with the United States" in what would become "the Taiwan of the Caribbean." The World Bank concurred, offering the usual prescriptions for "expansion of private enterprises" and minimization of "social objectives," thus increasing inequality and poverty and reducing health and educational levels. It may be noted, for what it is worth, that these standard prescriptions are offered side by side with sermons on the need to reduce inequality and poverty and improve health and educational levels. In the Haitian case, the consequences were the usual ones: profits for U.S. manufacturers and the Haitian super-rich, and a decline of 56 percent in Haitian wages through the 1980s—in short, an "economic miracle." Haiti remained Haiti, not Taiwan, which had followed a radically different course, as advisers must surely know.

It was the effort of Haiti's first democratic government to alleviate the growing disaster that called forth Washington's hostility and the military coup and terror that followed. With "democracy restored," USAID is withholding aid to ensure that cement and flour mills are privatized for the benefit of wealthy Haitians and foreign investors (Haitian "Civil Society," according to the orders that accompanied the restoration of democracy), while barring expenditures for health and education. Agribusiness receives ample funding, but no resources are made available for peasant agriculture and handicrafts, which provide the income of the overwhelming majority of the population. Foreign-owned assembly plants that employ workers (mostly women) at well below subsistence pay under horrendous working conditions benefit from cheap electricity, subsidized by the generous supervisor. But for the Haitian poor—the general population—there can be no subsidies for electricity, fuel, water, or food; these are prohibited by IMF rules on the principled grounds that they constitute "price control."

Before the "reforms" were instituted, local rice production supplied virtually all domestic needs, with important linkages to the domestic economy. Thanks to one-sided "liberalization," it now provides only 50 percent, with the predictable effects on the economy. Haiti must "reform," eliminating tariffs in accord with the stern principles of economic science—which, by some miracle of logic, exempt U.S. agribusiness; it continues to receive huge public subsidies, increased by the Reagan Administration to the point where they provided 40 percent of growers' gross incomes by 1987. The natural consequences are understood: a 1995 USAID report observes that the "export-driven trade and investment policy" that Washington mandates will "relentlessly squeeze the domestic rice farmer," who will be forced to turn to the more rational pursuit of agroexport for the benefit of U.S. investors, in accord with the principles of rational expectations theory.[32]

By such methods, the most impoverished country in the hemisphere has been turned into a leading purchaser of U.S.-produced rice, enriching publicly subsidized U.S. enterprises. Those lucky enough to have received a good Western education can doubtless explain that the benefits will trickle down to Haitian peasants and slum dwellers—ultimately.

The prize example tells us more about the meaning and implications of the victory for "democracy and open markets."

Haitians seem to understand the lessons, even if doctrinal managers in the West prefer a different picture. Parliamentary elections in April 1997 brought forth "a dismal 5 percent" of voters, the press reported, thus raising the question, "Did Haiti Fail U.S. Hope?"[33] We have sacrificed so much to bring them democracy, but they are ungrateful and unworthy. One can see why "realists" urge that we stay aloof from crusades of "global meliorism."

Similar attitudes hold throughout the hemisphere. Polls show that in Central America, politics elicits "boredom," "distrust," and "indifference" in proportions far outdistancing "interest" or "enthusiasm" among "an apathetic public...which feels itself a spectator in its democratic system" and has "general pessimism about the future." The first Latin America survey, sponsored by the EU, found much the same: "the survey's most alarming message," the Brazilian coordinator commented, was "the popular perception that only the elite had benefited from the transition to democracy."[34] Latin American scholars observe that the recent wave of democratization coincided with neoliberal economic reforms, which have been harmful for most people, leading to a cynical appraisal of formal democratic procedures. The introduction of similar programs in the richest country in the world has had similar effects, as already discussed.

Let us return to the prevailing doctrine that "America's victory in the cold war" was a victory for democracy and the free market. With regard to democracy, the doctrine is partially true, though we have to understand what is meant by "democracy": top-down control "to protect the minority of the opulent against the majority." What about the free market? Here too, we find that doctrine is far removed from reality, as the example of Haiti once again illustrates.

Consider again the case of NAFTA, an agreement intended to lock Mexico into an economic discipline that protects investors from the danger of a "democracy opening." It is not a "free trade agreement." Rather, it is highly protectionist, designed to impede East Asian and European competitors. Furthermore, it shares with the global agreements such antimarket principles as "intellectual property rights" restrictions of an extreme sort that rich societies never accepted during their period of development, but that they now intend to use to protect home-based corporations: to destroy the pharmaceutical industry in poorer countries, for example—and, incidentally, to block technological innovations, such as improved production processes for patented products allowed under the traditional patent regime. Progress is no more a desideratum than markets, unless it yields benefits for those who count.

There are also questions about the nature of "trade." Over half of U.S. trade with Mexico is reported to consist of intrafirm transactions, up about 15 percent since NAFTA. Already a decade ago, mostly U.S.-owned plants in northern Mexico, employing few workers and with virtually no linkages to the Mexican economy, produced more than 33 percent of the engine blocks used in U.S. cars, and 75 percent of other essential components. The post-NAFTA collapse of the Mexican economy in 1994, exempting only the very rich and U.S. investors (protected by U.S. government bailouts), led to an increase of U.S.-Mexico trade as the new crisis, driving the population to still deeper misery, "transformed Mexico into a cheap [i.e., even cheaper] source of manufactured goods, with industrial wages one-tenth of those in the U.S.," the business press reports. According to some specialists, half of U.S. trade worldwide consists of such centrally managed transactions, and much the same is true of other industrial powers,[35] though one must treat with caution conclusions about institutions with limited public accountability. Some economists have plausibly described the world system as one of "corporate mercantilism," remote from the ideal of free trade. The OECD concludes that "oligopolistic competition and strategic interaction among firms and governments rather than the invisible hand of market forces condition today's competitive advantage and international division of labor in high-technology industries,"[36] implicitly adopting a similar view.

Even the basic structure of the domestic economy violates the neoliberal principles that are hailed. The main theme of the standard work on U.S. business history is that "modern business enterprise took the place of market mechanisms in coordinating the activities of the economy and allocating its resources," handling many transactions internally, another large departure from market principles.[37] There are many others. Consider, for example, the fate of Adam Smith's principle that the free movement of people—across borders, for example—is an essential component of free trade. When we move on to the world of transnational corporations, with strategic alliances and critical support from powerful states, the gap between doctrine and reality becomes substantial.

Public statements have to be interpreted in the light of these realities, among them Clinton's call for trade-not-aid for Africa, with a series of provisions that just happen to benefit U.S. investors and uplifting rhetoric that manages to avoid such matters as the long record of such approaches and the fact that the United States already had the most miserly aid program of any developed country even before the grand innovation. Or to take the obvious model, consider Chester Crocker's outline of Reagan Administration plans for Africa in 1981. "We support open market opportunities, access to key resources, and expanding African and American economies," he said, and want to bring African countries "into the mainstream of the free market economy."[38] The statement may seem to surpass cynicism, coming from the leaders of the "sustained assault" against the "free market economy." But Crocker's rendition is fair enough, when it is passed through the prism of really existing market doctrine. The market opportunities and access to resources are for foreign investors and their local associates, and the economies are to expand in a specific way, protecting "the minority of the opulent against the majority." The opulent, meanwhile, merit state protection and public subsidy. How else can they flourish, for the benefit of all?

Of course, the United States is not alone in its conceptions of "free trade," even if its ideologues often lead the cynical chorus. The gap between rich and poor countries from 1960 is substantially attributable to protectionist measures of the rich, a UN development report concluded in 1992. The 1994 report concluded that "the industrial countries, by violating the principles of free trade, are costing the developing countries an estimated $50 billion a year—nearly equal to the total flow of foreign assistance"— much of it publicly subsidized export promotion.[39] The 1996 *Global Report* of the UN Industrial Development Organization estimates that the disparity between the richest and poorest 20 percent of the world population increased by over 50 percent from 1960 to 1989, and predicts "growing world inequality resulting from the globalization process." That growing disparity holds within the rich societies as well, the United States leading the way, Britain not far behind. The business press exults in "spectacular" and "stunning" profit growth, applauding the extraordinary concentration of wealth among the top few percent of the population, while for the majority, conditions continue to stagnate or decline.

The corporate media, the Clinton Administration, and the cheerleaders for the American Way proudly offer themselves as a model for the rest of the world; buried in the chorus of self-acclaim are the results of deliberate social policy of recent years, for example, the "basic indicators" just published by UNICEF,[40] revealing that the United States has the worst record among the industrial countries, ranking alongside Cuba—a poor third world country under unremitting attack by the hemispheric superpower for almost forty years—by such standards as mortality for children under five. It also holds records for hunger, child poverty, and other basic social indicators.

All of this takes place in the richest country in the world, with unparalleled advantages and stable democratic institutions, but also under business rule, to an unusual extent. These are further auguries for the future, if the "dramatic shift away from a pluralist, participatory ideal of politics and towards an authoritarian and technocratic ideal" proceeds on course, worldwide.

It is worth noting that in secret, intentions are often spelled out honestly. For example, in the early post-World War II period, George Kennan, one of the most influential planners and considered a leading humanist, assigned each sector of the world its "function": Africa's function was to be "exploited" by Europe for its reconstruction, he observed, the United States having little interest in it. A year earlier, a high-level planning study had urged "that cooperative development of the cheap foodstuffs and raw materials of northern Africa could help forge European unity and create an economic base for continental recovery," an interesting concept of "cooperation."[41] There is no record of a suggestion that Africa might "exploit" the West for its recovery from the "global meliorism" of the past centuries.

In this review, I have tried to follow a reasonable methodological principle: to evaluate the praise for the "political and economic principles" of the world dominant power by keeping primarily to illustrations selected by the advocates themselves, as their strongest cases. The review is brief and partial, and deals with matters that are obscure and not well understood. My own judgment, for what it is worth, is that the sample is fair enough, and that it yields a sobering picture of the operative principles as well as of the likely "wave of the future" if they prevail unchallenged.

Even if accurate, the picture is seriously misleading, precisely because it is so partial: missing entirely are the achievements of those who really are committed to the fine principles proclaimed, and to principles of justice and freedom that reach far beyond. This is primarily a record of popular struggle seeking to erode and dismantle forms of oppression and domination, which sometimes are all too apparent but are often so deeply entrenched as to be virtually invisible, even to their victims. The record is rich and encouraging, and we have every reason to suppose that it can be carried forward. To do so requires a realistic assessment of existing circumstances and their historical origins, but that is of course only a bare beginning.

Skeptics who dismiss such hopes as utopian and naive have only to cast their eyes on what has happened right here in South Africa in the last few years, a tribute to what the human spirit can accomplish, and its limitless prospects. The lessons of these remarkable achievements should be an inspiration to people everywhere, and should guide the next steps in the continuing struggle here too, as the people of South Africa, fresh from one great victory, turn to the still more difficult challenges that lie ahead.

Notes

1. UNICEF, *The State of the World's Children 1997* (Oxford University Press, 1997); UNICEF, *The Progress of Nations 1996* (UNICEF House, 1996).

2. Thomas Friedman, *NYT*, June 2, 1992; National Security Adviser Anthony Lake, *NYT*, September 26, 1993; historian David Fromkin, *NYT Book Review*, May 4, 1997, summarizing recent work.

3. On the general picture and its historical origins, see, inter alia, Frederic Clairmont's classic study, *The Rise and Fall of Economic Liberalism* (Asia Publishing House, 1960), reprinted and updated (Penang and Goa: Third World Network, 1996); and Michel Chossudovsky, *The Globalisation of Poverty* (Penang: Third World Network, 1997). Clairmont was an UNCTAD economist for many years; Chossudovsky is professor of economics at the University of Ottawa.

4. John Cassidy, *New Yorker*, October 16, 1995. See Chapter. 3, note 1, for quotes that follow. The sample is liberal-to-left, in some cases quite critical. The analysis is similar across the rest of the spectrum, but generally euphoric.

5. John Liscio, *Barron's*, April 15, 1996.

6. Richard Cockett, "The Party, Publicity, and the Media," in Anthony Seldon and Stuart Ball, eds., *Conservative Century: The Conservative Party since 1900* (Oxford University Press, 1994); Harold Lasswell, "Propaganda," in *Encyclopaedia of the Social Sciences*, vol. 12 (Macmillan, 1933). For quotes and discussion, see "Intellectuals and the State" (1977), reprinted in Noam Chomsky, *Towards a New Cold War* (Pantheon, 1982). Also at last available is some of the pioneering work on these topics by Alex Carey, collected in his *Taking the Risk out of Democracy* (University of New South Wales Press, 1995, and University of Illinois Press, 1997).

7. *Ibid.*, and Elizabeth Fones-Wolf, *Selling Free Enterprise: the Business Assault on Labor and Liberalism, 1945-1960* (University of Illinois Press, 1995). Also Stuart Ewen, *PR!: A Social History of SPIN* (Basic Books, 1996). On the broader context, see Noam Chomsky, "Intellectuals and the State" and "Force and Opinion," reprinted in *Deterring Democracy* (Verso, 1991).

8. Editorial, *New Republic*, March 19, 1990.

9. Sanford Lakoff, *Democracy: History, Theory, Practice* (Westview, 1996), 262 f.

10. J. Toye, J. Harrigan, and P. Mosley, *Aid and Power* (Routledge, 1991), vol. 1, 16. On the Leninist comparison, see my essays cited in note 7 and *For Reasons of State* (Pantheon, 1973), Introduction.

11. Carothers, "The Reagan Years," in Abraham Lowenthal, ed., *Exporting Democracy* (Johns Hopkins University Press, 1991). See also his *In the Name of Democracy* (University of California Press, 1991).

12. See Chapter 2, and for further discussion and sources, Noam Chomsky, *Powers and Prospects* (South End, 1996), "'Consent Without Consent': Reflections on the Theory and Practice of Democracy," *Cleveland State Law Review* 44.4, 1996.

13. *Survey of Current Business*, U.S. Dept. of Commerce, Vol. 76, no. 12 (December 1966).

14. Morton Horwitz, *The Transformation of American Law, 1870-1960* (Harvard University Press, 1992), Chapter 3. See also Charles Sellers, *The Market Revolution* (Oxford University Press, 1991).

15. Michael Sandel, *Democracy's Discontent* (Harvard University Press, 1996), Chapter 6. His interpretation in terms of republicanism and civic virtue is too narrow, in my opinion, overlooking deeper roots in the Enlightenment and before. For some discussion, see among others Noam Chomsky, *Problems of Knowledge and Freedom* (Pantheon, 1971), Chapter 1; several essays reprinted in James Peck, ed., *The Chomsky Reader* (Pantheon,

1987); and Noam Chomsky, *Powers and Prospects*, Chapter 4.

16. For details, see Noam Chomsky, *Turning the Tide* (Boston: South End, 1985), Chapter 6.3; and Noam Chomsky, *The Culture of Terrorism* (South End, 1988), Chapter 11 (and sources cited), including quotes from Figueres, whose exclusion from the media took considerable dedication. See my *Letters from Lexington* (Common Courage, 1993), Chapter 6, on the record, including the long obituary in the *New York Times* by its Central America specialist and the effusive accompanying editorial, which again succeeded in completely banning his views on Washington's "crusade for democracy." On media coverage of Nicaraguan and Salvadoran elections, see Edward Herman and Noam Chomsky, *Manufacturing Consent* (Pantheon, 1988), Chapter 3. Even Carothers, who is careful with the facts, writes that the Sandinistas "refused to agree to elections" until 1990 (in Lowenthal, *op. cit.*).

17. Another standard falsification is that the long-planned elections took place only because of Washington's military and economic pressures, which are therefore retroactively justified.

18. On the elections and the reaction in Latin America and the United States, including sources for what follows, see Noam Chomsky, *Deterring Democracy*, Chapter 10. For a detailed review of the very successful subversion of diplomacy, hailed generally as a triumph of diplomacy, see Noam Chomsky, *Culture of Terrorism*, Chapter 7; and Noam Chomsky, *Necessary Illusions* (South End, 1989), appendix IV.5.

19. His emphasis, in Lowenthal, *op. cit.*

20. For details, see, inter alia, Richard Garfield, "Desocializing Health Care in a Developing Country," *Journal of the American Medical Association*, 270, no. 8, August 25, 1993, and Noam Chomsky, *World Orders, Old and New* (Columbia University Press, 1994), 131 f.

21. Michael Kinsley, *Wall Street Journal*, March 26, 1987; *New Republic*, editorials, April 2, 1984; March 19, 1990. For more on these and many similar examples, see Noam Chomsky, *Culture of Terrorism*, Chapter 5; Chomsky, *Deterring Democracy*, Chapters 10, 12.

22. H.D.S. Greenway, *Boston Globe*, July 29, 1993.

23. *NYT*, May 2, 1985.

24. See *World Orders*, 131 ff. On the predictions and the outcome, see economist Melvin Burke, "NAFTA Integration: Unproductive Finance and Real Unemployment," *Proceedings from the Eighth Annual Labor Segmentation Conference*, April 1995, sponsored by Notre Dame and Indi-

ana Universities. Also *Social Dimensions of North American Economic Integration*, report prepared for the Department of Human Resources Development by the Canadian Labour Congress, 1996. On World Bank predictions for Africa, see Cheryl Payer, *Lent and Lost* (Zed, 1991) and John Mihevc, *The Market Tells them So* (Zed, 1995), also reviewing the grim effects of consistent failure—grim for the population, that is, not for the Bank's actual constituency. That the record of prediction is poor, and understanding meager, is well known to professional economists. See, e.g., Paul Krugman, "Cycles of Conventional Wisdom on Economic Development," *International Affairs* 71 no. 4, October 1995. See 25f., above.

25. Helene Cooper, "Experts' View of NAFTAS's Economic Impact: It's a Wash," *WSJ*, June 17, 1997.

26. Editorial, "Class War in the USA," *Multinational Monitor*, March 1997. Bronfenbrenner, "We'll Close," *ibid.*, based on the study she directed: "Final Report: The Effects of Plant Closing or Threat of Plant Closing on the Right of Workers to Organize." The massive impact of Reaganite criminality is detailed in a report in *Business Week*, "The Workplace: Why America Needs Unions, But Not The Kind It Has Now," May 23, 1994.

27. Levinson, *Foreign Affairs*, March/April 1996. Workshop, September 26 & 27, 1990, Minutes, 3.

28. See next chapter. In the U.S. and particularly Canada (where there was far more open discussion), the population remained largely opposed, polls indicated.

29. Kenneth Roth, Executive Director, HRW, Letter, *NYT*, April 12, 1997.

30. See Paul Farmer, *The Uses of Haiti* (Common Courage, 1994); Chomsky, *World Orders*, 62 ff.; Noam Chomsky, "Democracy Restored," Z, November 1994; North American Congress on Latin America (NACLA), *Haiti: Dangerous Crossroads* (South End, 1995).

31. Noam Chomsky, "Democracy Restored," citing John Solomon, AP, September 18, 1994 (lead story).

32. See my *Year 501* (South End, 1993), Chapter 8, and sources cited; Farmer, *op. cit. Labor Rights in Haiti*, International Labor Rights Education and Research Fund, April 1989. *Haiti After the Coup*, National Labor Committee Education Fund (New York), April 1993. Lisa McGowan, *Democracy Undermined, Economic Justice Denied: Structural Adjustment and the AID Juggernaut in Haiti* (Development Gap, January 1997).

33. Nick Madigan, "Democracy in Inaction: Did Haiti Fail U.S. Hope?" *Christian Science Monitor*, April 8, 1997; See AP, *Boston Globe*, April 8, 1997, for more on the elections.

34. John McPhaul, *Tico Times* (Costa Rica), April 11; May 2, 1997.

35. Vincent Cable, *Daedalus* (Spring 1995), citing UN *World Investment Report 1993* (which, however, gives quite different figures, noting also that "relatively little data are available" 164 f.). For more detailed discussion, estimating intra-TNC trade at 40 percent, see Peter Cowhey and Jonathan Aronson, *Managing the World Economy* (New York, Council on Foreign Relations, 1993). On U.S.-Mexico, see David Barkin and Fred Rosen, "Why the Recovery is Not a Recovery," *NACLA Report on the Americas*, January/February 1997; Leslie Crawford, "Legacy of Shock Therapy," *Financial Times*, February 12, 1997 (subtitled "Mexico: A Healthier Outlook," the article reviews the increasing misery of the vast majority of the population, apart from "the very rich"). Post-NAFTA intrafirm transactions: William Greider, *One World, Ready or Not* (Simon & Schuster, 1997), 273, citing Mexican economist Carlos Heredia. Pre-NAFTA estimates of intrafirm U.S. exports never entering Mexican markets passed 50percent. Senator Ernest Hollings, *Foreign Policy*, Winter 1993-4.

36. 1992 OECD study cited by Clinton's former chief economic adviser Laura Tyson in *Who's Bashing Whom?* (Institute for International Economics, 1992).

37. Alfred Chandler, *The Visible Hand* (Belknap Press, 1977).

38. Speech delivered by C. A. Crocker, Assistant Secretary of State for African Affairs, in Honolulu before the National Security Committee of the American Legion, August 1981. Cited by Hans Abrahamsson, *Hegemony, Region and Nation State: The Case of Mozambique* (Padrigu Peace and Development Research Institute, Gothenburg University, January 1996).

39. For discussion, see Eric Toussaint and Peter Drucker, eds., *IMF/World Bank/WTO, Notebooks for Study and Research* (Amsterdam: International Institute for Research and Education, 1995), 24/5.

40. UNICEF, *State of the World's Children 1997*.

41. George Kennan, PPS 23, February 24, 1948 (*Foreign Relations of the United States*, vol. 1, 1948), 511. Michael Hogan, *The Marshall Plan* (Cambridge University Press, 1987), 41, paraphrasing the May 1947 Bonesteel Memorandum.

V

The Zapatista Uprising

Major changes have taken place in the global order in the past quarter century. By 1970 the "affluent alliance" of the postwar years was running on to the rocks, and there was growing pressure on corporate profits. Recognizing that the United States was no longer able to play the role of "international banker" that had been so beneficial to U.S.-based multinationals, Richard Nixon dismantled the international economic order (the Bretton Woods system), suspending the convertibility of the dollar to gold, imposing wage-price controls and an import surcharge, and initiating fiscal measures that directed state power, beyond the previous norm, to welfare for the rich. These have been the guiding policies since, accelerated during the Reagan years and maintained by the "New Democrats." The unremitting class war waged by business sectors was intensified, increasingly on a global scale.

Nixon's moves were among several factors that led to a huge increase in unregulated financial capital and a radical shift in its use, from long-term investment and trade to speculation. The effect has been to undermine national economic planning as governments are compelled to preserve market "credibility," driving many economies "toward a low-growth, high-unemployment equilibrium," Cambridge University economist John Eatwell comments, with stagnating or declining real wages, increasing poverty and inequality, and booming markets and profits for the few. The parallel process of internationalization of production provides new weapons to undermine working people in the West, who must accept an end to their "luxurious" lifestyle and agree to "flexibility of labor markets" (not knowing whether you have a job tomorrow), the business press orates happily. The return of most of Eastern Europe to its third world origins enhances these prospects considerably. The attack on workers' rights, social standards, and functioning democracy throughout the world reflects these victories.

The triumphalism among narrow elite sectors is quite understandable, as is the despair and anger outside privileged circles.

The New Year's Day uprising of Indian peasants in Chiapas can readily be understood in this general context. The uprising coincided with the enactment of NAFTA, which the Zapatista army called a "death sentence" for Indians, a gift to the rich that will deepen the divide between narrowly concentrated wealth and mass misery, and destroy what remains of the indigenous society.

The NAFTA connection is partly symbolic; the problems are far deeper. "We are the product of 500 years of struggle," the Zapatistas' declaration of war stated. The struggle today is "for work, land, housing, food, health care, education, independence, freedom, democracy, justice, and peace." "The real background," the vicar-general of the Chiapas diocese added, "is complete marginalization and poverty and the frustration of many years trying to improve the situation."

The Indian peasants are the most aggrieved victims of Mexican government policies. But their distress is widely shared. "Anyone who has the opportunity to be in contact with the millions of Mexicans who live in extreme poverty knows that we are living with a time bomb," Mexican columnist Pilar Valdes observed.

In the past decade of economic reform, the number of people living in extreme poverty in rural areas increased by almost a third. Half the total population lacks resources to meet basic needs, a dramatic increase since 1980. Following International Monetary

Fund (IMF)-World Bank prescriptions, agricultural production was shifted to export and animal feeds, benefiting agribusiness, foreign consumers, and affluent sectors in Mexico while malnutrition became a major health problem, agricultural employment declined, productive lands were abandoned, and Mexico began to import massive amounts of food. Real wages in manufacturing fell sharply. Labor's share in gross domestic product, which had risen until the mid-1970s, has since declined by well over a third. These are standard concomitants of neoliberal reforms. IMF studies show "a strong and consistent pattern of reduction of labor share of income" under the impact of its "stabilization programs" in Latin America, economist Manuel Pastor observes.

The Mexican Secretary of Commerce hailed the fall in wages as an inducement to foreign investors. So it is, along with repression of labor, lax enforcement of environmental restrictions, and the general orientation of social policy to the desires of the privileged minority. Such policies are naturally welcomed by the manufacturing and financial institutions that are extending their control over the global economy, with the assistance of mislabeled "free trade" agreements.

NAFTA is expected to drive large numbers of farm workers off the land, contributing to rural misery and surplus labor. Manufacturing employment, which declined under the reforms, is expected to fall more sharply. A study by Mexico's leading business journal, *El Financiero*, predicted that Mexico would lose almost a quarter of its manufacturing industry and 14 percent of its jobs in the first two years. "Economists predict that several million Mexicans will probably lose their jobs in the first five years after the accord takes effect," Tim Golden reported in the *New York Times*. These processes should depress wages still further while increasing profits and polarization, with predictable effects in the United States and Canada.

A large part of the appeal of NAFTA, as its more forthright advocates regularly stressed, is that it "locks in" the neoliberal reforms that have reversed years of progress in labor rights and economic development, bringing mass impoverishment and suffering along with enrichment for the few and for foreign investors. To Mexico's economy generally, this "economic virtue" has brought "little reward," the London *Financial Times* observes, reviewing "eight years of textbook market economic policies" that produced little growth, most of it attributable to unparalleled financial assistance from the World Bank and the United States. High interest rates have partially reversed the huge capital flight that was a major factor in Mexico's debt crisis, though debt service is a growing burden, its largest component now being the internal debt owed to the Mexican rich.

Not surprisingly, there was substantial opposition to the plan to "lock in" this model of development. Historian Seth Fein, writing from Mexico City, described large demonstrations against NAFTA, "well articulated, if too-little-noticed in the United States, cries of frustration against government policies—involving repeal of constitutional labor, agrarian, and education rights stipulated in the nation's popularly revered 1917 constitution—that appear to many Mexicans as the real meaning of NAFTA and U.S. foreign policy here." *Los Angeles Times* correspondent Juanita Darling reported the great anxiety of Mexican workers about the erosion of their "hard-won labor rights," likely to "be sacrificed as companies, trying to compete with foreign companies, look for ways to cut costs."

A "Communication of Mexican Bishops on NAFTA" condemned the agreement along with the economic policies of which it is a part because of their deleterious social effects. The bishops reiterated the concern of the 1992 conference of Latin American bishops that "the market economy does not become something absolute to which everything is sacrificed, accentuating the inequality and the marginalization of a large portion of the population"—the likely impact of NAFTA and similar investor rights agreements. The reaction of the Mexican business world was mixed: the most powerful elements favored the agreement, while mid-sized and small businesses, and their organizations, were dubious or hostile. The leading Mexican journal *Excelsior* predicted that

NAFTA would benefit only "those 'Mexicans' who are today the masters of almost the entire country (15 percent receive more than half the GDP)," a "de-Mexicanized minority," and would be another stage of "the history of the United States in our country," "one of unchecked abuses and looting." The agreement was also opposed by many workers (including the largest nongovernmental union) and other groups, which warned of the impact on wages, workers' rights, and the environment, the loss of sovereignty, the increased protection for corporate and investor rights, and the undermining of options for sustainable growth. Homero Aridjis, president of Mexico's leading environmental organization, deplored "the third conquest that Mexico has suffered. The first was by arms, the second was spiritual, the third is economic."

It did not take long for such fears to be realized. Shortly after the NAFTA vote in Congress, workers were fired from Honeywell and GE plants for attempting to organize independent unions. The Ford Motor Company had fired its entire work force in 1987, eliminating the union contract and rehiring workers at far lower salaries. Forceful repression suppressed protests. Volkswagen followed suit in 1992, firing its 14,000 workers and rehiring only those who renounced independent union leaders, with government backing. These are central components of the "economic miracle" that is to be "locked in" by NAFTA.

A few days after the NAFTA vote, the U.S. Senate passed "the finest anticrime package in history" (Senator Orrin Hatch), calling for 100,000 new police, high-security regional prisons, boot camps for young offenders, extension of the death penalty and harsher sentencing, and other onerous conditions. Law enforcement experts interviewed by the press doubted that the legislation would have much effect on crime because it did not deal with the "causes of social disintegration that produce violent criminals." Primary among these are the social and economic policies polarizing American society, carried another step forward by NAFTA. The concepts of "efficiency" and "health of the economy" preferred by wealth and privilege offer nothing to the growing sectors of the population that are useless for profit-making, driven to poverty and despair. If they cannot be confined to urban slums, they will have to be controlled in some other way.

Like the timing of the Zapatista rebellion, the legislative coincidence was of more than mere symbolic significance.

The NAFTA debate focused largely on job flows, about which little is understood. But a more confident expectation is that wages will be held down rather broadly. "Many economists think NAFTA could drag down pay," Steven Pearlstein reported in the *Washington Post,* expecting that "lower Mexican wages could have a gravitational effect on the wages of Americans." That is expected even by NAFTA advocates, who recognize that less skilled work-ers—about 70 percent of the work force—are likely to suffer wage loss.

The day after the congressional vote approving NAFTA, the *New York Times* ran its first review of the expected effects of the treaty on the New York region. The review was upbeat, consis-tent with the enthusiastic support throughout. It focused on the expected gainers: sectors "based in and around finance," "the region's banking, telecommunications, and service firms," insurance companies, investment houses, corporate law firms, the PR indus-try, management consultants, and the like. It predicted that some manufacturers might gain, primarily in high tech industry, pub-lishing, and pharmaceuticals, which will benefit from the protec-tionist measures designed to ensure that major corporations control the technology of the future. In passing, the review mentioned that there will also be losers, "predominantly women, blacks and His-panics," and "semi-skilled production workers" generally: that is, most of the population of a city where 40 percent of children already live below the poverty line, suffering health and educa-tional disabilities that "lock them in" to a bitter fate.

Noting that real wages have fallen to the level of the 1960s for production and nonsupervisory workers, the Congressional Office of Technology Assessment, in its analysis of the planned (and implemented) version of NAFTA, predicted that it "could further lock the United States into a low-wage, low-productivity future," though revisions proposed by OTA, labor, and other critics—never admitted to the debate—could benefit the populations in all three countries.

The version of NAFTA that was enacted is likely to accelerate a "welcome development of transcendent importance" (*Wall Street Journal*): the reduction of U.S. labor costs to below any major industrial country apart from England. In 1985, the U.S. ranked at the high end among the seven major state capitalist economies (G-7), as one would expect of the richest country in the world. In a more integrated economy, the impact is worldwide, as competitors must accommodate. GM can move to Mexico, or now to Poland, where it can find workers at a fraction of the cost of Western labor and be protected by high tariffs and other restrictions. Volkswagen can move to the Czech Republic to benefit from similar protection, taking the profits and leaving the government with the costs. Daimler-Benz can make similar arrangements in Alabama. Capital can move freely; workers and communities suffer the consequences. Meanwhile the huge growth of unregulated speculative capital imposes powerful pressures against stimulative government policies.

There are many factors driving global society towards a low-wage, low-growth, high-profit future, with increasing polarization and social disintegration. Another consequence is the fading of meaningful democratic processes as decision making is vested in private institutions and the quasi-governmental structures that are coalescing around them, what the *Financial Times* calls a "de facto world government" that operates in secret and without accountability.

These developments have little to do with economic liberalism, a concept of limited significance in a world in which a vast component of "trade" consists of centrally-managed intrafirm transactions (half of U.S. exports to Mexico pre-NAFTA, for example—"exports" that never enter the Mexican market). Meanwhile private power demands and receives protection from market forces, as in the past.

"The Zapatistas really struck a chord with a large segment of the Mexican populace," Mexican political scientist Eduardo Gallardo commented shortly after the rebellion, predicting that the effects would be wide-ranging, including steps toward breaking down the long-standing electoral dictatorship. Polls in Mexico backed that conclusion, reporting majority support for the reasons given by the Zapatistas for their rebellion. A similar chord was struck worldwide, including the rich industrial societies, where many people recognized the concerns of the Zapatistas to be not unlike their own, despite their very different circumstances. Support was further stimulated by imaginative Zapatista initiatives to reach out to wider sectors and to engage them in common or parallel efforts to take control of their lives and fate. The domestic and international solidarity was doubtless a major factor in deterring the anticipated brutal military repression, and has had a dramatic energizing effect on organizing and activism worldwide.

The protest of Indian peasants in Chiapas gives only a bare glimpse of "time bombs" waiting to explode, not only in Mexico.

Much of this article originally appeared in
In These Times, February 21, 1994.

VI

"The
Ultimate
Weapon"

Let's begin with some simple points, assuming conditions that now prevail—not, of course, the terminus of the unending struggle for freedom and justice.

There is a "public arena" in which, in principle, individuals can participate in decisions that involve the general society: how public revenues are obtained and used, what foreign policy will be, etc. In a world of nation-states, the public arena is primarily governmental, at various levels. Democracy functions insofar as individuals can participate meaningfully in the public arena, meanwhile running their own affairs, individually and collectively, without illegitimate interference by concentrations of power. Functioning democracy presupposes relative equality in access to resources—material, informational, and other—a truism as old as Aristotle. In theory, governments are instituted to serve their "domestic constituencies" and are to be subject to their will. A measure of functioning democracy, then, is the extent to which the theory approximates reality, and the "domestic constituencies" genuinely approximate the population.

In the state capitalist democracies, the public arena has been extended and enriched by long and bitter popular struggle.

Meanwhile concentrated private power has labored to restrict it. These conflicts form a good part of modern history. The most effective way to restrict democracy is to transfer decision making from the public arena to unaccountable institutions: kings and princes, priestly castes, military juntas, party dictatorships, or modern corporations. The decisions reached by the directors of GE affect the general society substantially, but citizens play no role in them, as a matter of principle (we may put aside transparent myth about market and stockholder "democracy").

Systems of unaccountable power do offer some choices to citizens. They can petition the king or the CEO, or join the ruling party. They can try to rent themselves to GE, or buy its products. They can struggle for rights within tyrannies, state and private, and in solidarity with others, can seek to limit or dismantle illegitimate power, pursuing traditional ideals, including those that animated the U.S. labor movement from its early origins: that those who work in the mills should own and run them.

The "corporatization of America" during the past century has been an attack on democracy—and on markets, part of the shift from something resembling "capitalism" to the highly administered markets of the modern state/corporate era. A current variant is called "minimizing the state," that is, transferring decision-making power from the public arena to somewhere else: "to the people," in the rhetoric of power; to private tyrannies, in the real world. All such measures are designed to limit democracy and to tame the "rascal multitude," as the population was called by the self-designated "men of best quality" during the first upsurge of democracy in the modern period, in seventeenth century England; the "responsible men," as they call themselves today. The basic problems persist, constantly taking new forms, calling forth new measures of control and marginalization, and leading to new forms of popular struggle.

The so-called "free trade agreements" are one such device of undermining democracy. They are designed to transfer decision making about people's lives and aspirations into the hands of private tyrannies that operate in secret and without public supervision or control. Not surprisingly, the public doesn't like them. The opposition is almost instinctive, a tribute to the care that is taken to insulate the rascal multitude from relevant information and understanding.

Much of the picture is tacitly conceded. We've just witnessed yet another illustration: the effort of the past months to pass "Fast Track" legislation that would permit the executive to negotiate trade agreements without congressional oversight and public awareness; a simple *yes* or *no* will do. "Fast Track" had near unanimous support within power systems, but as the *Wall Street Journal* ruefully observed, its opponents may have an "ultimate weapon": the majority of the population. The public continued to oppose the legislation despite the media barrage, foolishly believing that they ought to know what is happening to them and have a voice in determining it. Similarly, NAFTA was rammed through over public opposition, which remained firm despite the near unanimous and enthusiastic backing of state and corporate power, including their media, which refused even to allow the position of the prime opponents (the labor movement) to be expressed while denouncing them for various invented misdeeds.[1]

Fast Track was portrayed as a free trade issue, but that is inaccurate. The most ardent free trader would strongly oppose Fast Track if she or he happened to believe in democracy, the issue at stake. That aside, the planned agreements hardly qualify as free trade agreements any more than NAFTA or the GATT/WTO treaties, matters discussed elsewhere.

The official reason for Fast Track was articulated by Deputy U.S. Trade Representative Jeffrey Lang: "The basic principle of negotiations is that only one person [the President] can negotiate for the U.S."[2] The role of Congress is to rubber-stamp; the role of the public is to watch—preferably, to watch something else.

The "basic principle" is real enough, but its scope is narrow. It holds for *trade*, but not for other matters: human rights, for example. Here the principle is the opposite: members of Congress must be granted every opportunity to ensure that the United States maintains its record of nonratification of agreements, one of the worst in the world. The few enabling conventions even to reach Congress have been held up for years, and even the rare endorsements are burdened with conditions rendering them inoperative in the United States; they are "non self-executing" and have specific reservations.

Trade is one thing, torture and rights of women and children another.

The distinction holds more broadly. China is threatened with severe sanctions for failing to adhere to Washington's protectionist demands, or for interfering with its punishment of Libyans. But terror and torture elicit a different response: in this case, sanctions would be "counterproductive." They would hamper our efforts to extend our human rights crusade to suffering people in China and its domains, just as reluctance to train Indonesian military officers "diminishes our ability to positively influence [their] human rights policies and behavior," as the Pentagon recently explained. The missionary effort in Indonesia therefore must proceed, evading congressional orders. That is only reasonable. It suffices to recall how U.S. military training "paid dividends" in the early 1960s, and "encouraged" the military to carry out their necessary tasks, as Defense Secretary Robert McNamara informed Congress and the President after the huge army-led massacres of 1965, which left hundreds of thousands of corpses in a few months, a "staggering mass slaughter" (*New York Times*) that elicited unconstrained euphoria among the "men of best quality" (the *Times* included), and rewards for the "moderates" who had conducted it. McNamara had particular praise for the training of Indonesian military officers in U.S. universities, "very significant factors" in setting the "new Indonesian political elite" (the military) on the proper course.

In crafting its human rights policies for China, the administration might have also recalled the constructive advice of a Kennedy military mission to Colombia: "As necessary execute paramilitary, sabotage, and/or terrorist activities against known communist proponents" (a term that covers peasants, union organizers, human rights activists, etc.). The pupils learned the lessons well, compiling the worst human rights record of the 1990s in the hemisphere with increasing U.S. military aid and training.

Reasonable people can easily understand, then, that it would be counterproductive to press China too hard on such matters as torture of dissidents or atrocities in Tibet. That might even cause China to suffer the "harmful effects of a society isolated from American influence," the reason adduced by a group of corporate executives for removing the U.S. trade barriers that keep them from Cuban markets, where they could labor to restore the "helpful effects of American influence" that prevailed from the "liberation" 100 years ago through the Batista years, the same influences that have proven so benign in Haiti, El Salvador, and other contemporary paradises—by accident, yielding profits as well.[3]

Such subtle discriminations must be part of the armory of those who aspire to respectability and prestige. Having mastered them, we can see why investors' rights and human rights require such different treatment. The contradiction about the "basic principle" is only apparent.

Propaganda's Black Holes

It is always enlightening to seek out what is omitted in propaganda campaigns. Fast Track received enormous publicity. But several crucial issues disappeared into the black hole that is reserved for topics rated unfit for public consumption. One is the fact, already mentioned, that the issue was not trade agreements but rather democratic principle; and that in any event the agreements were not about *free* trade. Still more striking was that throughout the intense campaign, there appears to have been no public mention of the upcoming treaty that must have been at the forefront of concern: the Multilateral Agreement on Investment (MAI), a far more significant matter than bringing Chile into

NAFTA or other tidbits served up to illustrate why the President alone must negotiate trade agreements, without public interference.

The MAI has powerful support among financial and industrial institutions, which have been intimately involved in its planning from the outset: for example, the United States Council for International Business, which, in its own words, "advances the global interests of American business both at home and abroad." In January 1996 the Council even published *A Guide to the Multilateral Agreement on Investment*, available to its business constituencies and their circles, surely to the media. Even before Fast Track was brought to Congress, the Council requested the Clinton Administration to include the MAI under the then-pending legislation, the *Miami Herald* reported in July 1997—apparently the first mention of the MAI in the press, and a rare one; we return to details.[4]

Why then the silence during the Fast Track controversy, or about the MAI altogether? A plausible reason comes to mind. Few political and media leaders doubt that were the public to be informed, it would be less than overjoyed about the MAI. Opponents might once again brandish their "ultimate weapon," if the facts break through. It only makes sense, then, to conduct the MAI negotiations under a "veil of secrecy," to borrow the term used by the former Chief Justice of Australia's High Court, Sir Anthony Mason, condemning his government's decision to remove from public scrutiny the negotiations over "an agreement which could have a great impact on Australia if we ratify it."[5]

No similar voices were heard here. It would have been superfluous: the veil of secrecy was defended with much greater vigilance in our free institutions.

Within the United States, few know anything about the MAI, which has been under intensive negotiation in the OECD since May 1995. The original target date was May 1997. Had the goal been reached, the public would have known as much about the MAI as they do about the Telecommunications Act of 1996, another huge public gift to concentrated private power, kept largely to the business pages. But the OECD countries could not reach agreement on schedule, and the target date was delayed a year.

The original and preferred plan was to forge the treaty in the World Trade Organization. But that effort was blocked by third world countries, particularly India and Malaysia, which recognized that the measures being crafted would deprive them of the devices that had been employed by the rich to win their own place in the sun. Negotiations were then transferred to the safer quarters of the OECD, where, it was hoped, an agreement would be reached "that emerging countries would want to join," as the London *Economist* delicately put it [6]—on pain of being barred from the markets and resources of the rich, the familiar concept of "free choice" in systems of vast inequality of power and wealth.

For almost three years, the rascal multitude has been kept in blissful ignorance of what is taking place. But not entirely. In the third world it had become a live issue by early 1997.[7] In Australia, the news broke through in January 1998 in the business pages, eliciting a flurry of reports and controversy in the national press; hence Sir Anthony's condemnation, speaking at a convention in Melbourne. The opposition party "urged the government to refer the agreement to the Parliamentary committee on treaties before signing it," the press reported. The government refused to provide Parliament with detailed information or to permit parliamentary review. Our "position on the MAI is very clear," the government responded: "We will not sign anything unless it is demonstrably in Australia's national interest to do so." In brief, "We'll do as we choose"—or more accurately, as our masters tell us; and following the regular convention, the "national interest" will be defined by power centers, operating in closed chambers.

Under pressure, the government agreed a few days later to allow a parliamentary committee to review the MAI. Editors reluctantly endorsed the decision: it was necessary in reaction to the "xenophobic hysteria" of the "scaremongers" and the "unholy alliance of aid groups, trade unions, environmentalists and the odd conspiracy theorist." They warned, however, that after this unfortunate concession, it is "vitally important that the Government does not step back any further from its strong commitment" to the MAI. The government denied the charge of secrecy, noting that a draft of the treaty was available on the Internet—thanks to the activist groups that placed it there, after it was leaked to them.[8]

We can be heartened: democracy flourishes in Australia after all!

In Canada, now facing a form of incorporation into the United States accelerated by "free trade," the "unholy alliance" achieved much greater success. For a year, the treaty has been discussed in leading dailies and news weeklies, on prime time national TV, and in public meetings. The Province of British Columbia announced in the House of Commons that it "is strongly opposed" to the proposed treaty, noting its "unacceptable restrictions" on elected governments at the federal, provincial, and local levels; its harmful impact on social programs (health care, etc.) and on environmental protection and resource management; the extraordinary scope of the definition of "investment"; and other attacks on democracy and human rights. The provincial government was particularly opposed to provisions that allow corporations to sue governments while they remain immune from any liability, and to have their charges settled in "unelected and unaccountable dispute panels," which are to be constituted of "trade experts," operating without rules of evidence or transparency, and with no possibility of appeal.

The veil of secrecy having been shredded by the rude noises from below, it became necessary for the Canadian government to reassure the public that ignorance is in their best interest. The task was undertaken in a national CBC TV debate by Canada's Federal Minister of International Trade, Sergio Marchi: he "would like to think that people feel reassured," he said, by the "honest approach that I think is exuded by our Prime Minister" and "the love of Canada that he has."

That ought to settle the matter. So democracy is healthy north of the border too.

According to CBC, the Canadian government—like Australia—"has no plans at this time for any legislation on the MAI," and "the trade minister says it may not be necessary," since the MAI "is just an extension of NAFTA.[9]

There has been discussion in the national media in England and France, but I do not know whether there or elsewhere in the free world it was felt necessary to assure the public that their interests are best served by faith in the leaders who "love them," "exude honesty," and steadfastly defend "the national interest."

Not too surprisingly, the tale has followed a unique course in the world's most powerful state, where "the men of best quality" declare themselves the champions of freedom, justice, human rights, and—above all—democracy. Media leaders have surely known all along about the MIA and its broad implications, as have public intellectuals and the standard experts. As already noted, the business world was both aware and actively involved. But in a most impressive show of self-discipline, with exceptions that amount to statistical error, the free press has succeeded in keeping those who rely on it in the dark—no simple task in a complicated world.

The corporate world overwhelmingly supports the MAI. Though silence precludes citation of evidence, it is a fair guess that the sectors of the corporate world devoted to enlightening the public are no less enthusiastic. But once again, they understand that the "ultimate weapon" may well be unsheathed if the rascal multitude gets wind of the proceedings. The dilemma has a natural solution. We've been observing it now for almost three years.

Worthy and Unworthy Constituencies

Defenders of the MAI have one strong argument: critics do not have enough information to make a fully convincing case. The purpose of the "veil of secrecy" has been to guarantee that outcome, and the efforts have had some success. That is most dramatically true in the United States, which enjoys the world's most stable and long-lasting democratic institutions and can properly claim to be the model for state-capitalist democracy. Given this experience and status, it is not surprising that the principles of democracy are clearly understood in the United States, and lucidly articulated in high places. For example, the distinguished Harvard political scientist Samuel Huntington, in his text *American Politics*, observes that power must remain invisible if it is to be effective: "The architects of power in the United States must create a force that can be felt but not seen. Power remains strong when it remains in the dark; exposed to the sunlight it begins to evaporate." He illustrated the thesis in the same year (1981) while explaining the function of the "Soviet threat": "You may have to sell [intervention or other military action] in such a way as to create the misimpression that it is the Soviet Union that you are fighting. That is what the United States has been doing ever since the Truman Doctrine."[10]

Within these bounds—"creating misimpression" to delude the public, and excluding them entirely—responsible leaders are to pursue their craft in democratic societies.

Nonetheless, it is unfair to charge the OECD powers with conducting the negotiations in secret. After all, activists did succeed in putting a draft version on the Internet, having illicitly obtained it. Readers of the "alternative press" and third world journals, and those infected by the "unholy alliance," have been following the proceedings since early 1997 at least. And keeping to the mainstream, there is no gainsaying the direct participation of the organization that "advances the global interests of American businesses," and their counterparts in other rich countries.

But there are a few sectors that have somehow been overlooked: the U.S. Congress, for example. Last November, twenty-five House representatives sent a letter to President Clinton stating that the MAI negotiations had "come to our attention"—presumably through the efforts of activists and public interest groups.[11] They asked the president to answer three simple questions.

First, "Given the Administration's recent claims that it cannot negotiate complicated, multisectoral, multilateral agreements without fast track authority, how has the MAI nearly been completed," with a text "as intricate as NAFTA or GATT" and with provisions that "would require significant limitations on U.S. laws and policy concerning federal, state, and local regulation of investment?"

Second, "How has this agreement been under negotiation since May 1995, without any Congressional consultation or oversight, especially given Congress' exclusive constitutional authority to regulate international commerce?"

Third, "The MAI provides expansive takings language that would allow a foreign corporation or investor to directly sue the U.S. government for damages if we take any action that would restrain 'enjoyment' of an investment. This language is broad and vague and goes significantly beyond the limited concept of takings provided in U.S. domestic law. Why would the U.S. willingly cede sovereign immunity and expose itself to liability for damages under vague language such as that concerning taking any actions 'with an equivalent effect' of an 'indirect' expropriation?"

On point three, the signatories might have had in mind the suit by the Ethyl Corporation—famous as the producer of leaded gasoline—against Canada, demanding $250 million to cover losses from "expropriation" and damages to Ethyl's "good reputation" caused by Canadian legislation to ban MMT, a gasoline additive. Canada regards MMT as a dangerous toxin and significant health risk, in agreement with the U.S. Environmental Protection Agency, which has sharply restricted its use, and the state of California, which has banned it entirely. The suit also demands damages for the "chilling effect" of Canada's law, which has caused New Zealand and other countries to review their use of MMT, Ethyl charges. Or perhaps the signers were thinking of the suit against Mexico by the U.S. hazardous-waste management firm Metalclad, asking $90 million in damages for "expropriation" because a site they intended to use for hazardous wastes was declared part of an ecological zone.[12]

These suits are proceeding under NAFTA rules, which permit corporations to sue governments, according them in effect the rights of national states (not mere persons, as before). The intention presumably is to explore and if possible expand the (vague) limits of these rules. In part they are probably just intimidation, a standard and often effective device available to those with deep pockets to obtain what they want through legal threats that may be completely frivolous.[13]

"Considering the enormity of the MAI's potential implications," the congressional letter to the president concluded, "we eagerly await your answers to these questions." An answer finally reached the signers, saying nothing. The media were advised of all of this, but I know of no coverage.[14]

Another group that has been overlooked, along with Congress, is the population. Apart from trade journals, there was, to my knowledge, no coverage in the mainstream press until mid-1997, and there has been virtually none since. As mentioned, the *Miami Herald* reported the MAI in July 1997, noting the enthusiasm and direct involvement of the business world. The *Chicago Tribune* carried a report in December, observing that the matter has "received no public attention or political debate," apart from Canada. In the United States, "this obscurity seems deliberate," the *Tribune* reports. "Government sources say the administration…is not anxious to stir up more debate about the global economy." In the light of the public mood, secrecy is the best policy, relying on the collusion of the information system.

The Newspaper of Record broke its silence a few months later, publishing a paid advertisement by the International Forum on Globalization, which opposes the treaty. The ad quotes a headline in *Business Week*, which describes the MAI as "the explosive trade deal you've never heard of." "The accord…would rewrite the rules of foreign ownership—affecting everything from factories to real estate and even securities. But most lawmakers have never even heard of the Multilateral Agreement on Investment because secretive talks by the Clinton Administration have been carried out beneath congressional radar," and the media have kept to the White House agenda. Why? the International Forum asks, implicitly answering with a review of the basic features of the treaty.

A few days later (February 16, 1998), NPR's *Morning Edition* ran a segment on the MAI. A week later, the *Christian Science Monitor* ran a (rather thin) piece. The *New Republic* had already taken notice of rising public concern over the MAI. The issue had not been properly covered in respectable sectors, The *New Republic* concluded, because "the mainstream press," while "generally skewed to the left…is even more deeply skewed toward internationalism." Press lefties therefore failed to recognize the public opposition to Fast Track in time and have not noticed that the same troublemakers "are already girding [for] battle" against the MAI. The press should confront its responsibilities more seriously and launch a preemptive strike against the "MAI paranoia" that has "ricocheted through the Internet" and even led to public conferences. Mere ridicule of "the flat earth and black helicopter crowd" may not be enough. Silence may not be the wisest stance if the rich countries are to be able to "lock in the liberalization of international investment law just as GATT codified the liberalization of trade."

On April 1, 1998, the *Washington Post* brought the news to a national audience in an opinion piece by editorial staffer Fred Hiatt. He offers the ritual derision of critics and of the claim of "secrecy"—the text was, after all, placed (illicitly) on the Web by activists. Like others who sink to this level of apologetics, he fails to draw the obvious consequences: that the media should gracefully exit the stage. Any meaningful evidence they use could be discovered by ordinary folk with diligent search, and analysis/commentary/debate are declared irrelevant.

Hiatt writes that the "MAI hasn't yet attracted much attention in Washington" —in particular, in his journal—a year after the first date for signing passed, and three weeks before the 1998 target date. He limits his coverage to a few vacuous official comments, presented as unquestioned fact, and adds that the government has "learned from fast-track that they have to consult, while treaties are still being shaped, more than ever before—unions, local officials, environmentalists as others." As we have observed.[15]

Perhaps in reaction to the congressional letter or the surfacing of the crazies, Washington issued an official statement on the MAI on February 17, 1998. The statement, by Undersecretary of State Stuart Eizenstat and Deputy U.S. Trade Representative Jeffrey Lang, received no notice to my knowledge. The statement is boilerplate, but deserves front-page headlines by the standards of what had already appeared (essentially nothing). The virtues of the MAI are taken as self-evident; no description or argument is offered. On such matters as labor and the environment, "takings," etc., the message is the same as the one delivered by the governments of Canada and Australia: "Trust us, and shut up."

Of greater interest is the good news that the United States has taken the lead at the OECD in ensuring that the agreement "complements our broader efforts," hitherto unknown, "in support of sustainable development and promotion of respect for labor standards." Eizenstat and Lang "are pleased that participants agree with us" on these matters. Furthermore, the other OECD countries now "agree with us on the importance of working closely with their domestic constituencies to build a consensus" on the MAI. They join us in understanding "that it is important for domestic constituencies to have a stake in this process."

"In the interest of greater transparency," the official statement adds, "the OECD has agreed to make public the text of the draft agreement," perhaps even before the deadline is reached.[16]

Here we have, at last, a ringing testimonial to democracy and human rights. The Clinton Administration is leading the world, it proclaims, in ensuring that its "domestic constituencies" play an active role in "building a consensus" on the MAI.

Who are the "domestic constituencies"? The question is readily answered by a look at the uncontested facts. The business world has had an active role throughout. Congress was not informed, and the annoying public—the "ultimate weapon"—was consigned to ignorance. A straightforward exercise in elementary logic informs us exactly who the Clinton Administration takes to be its "domestic constituencies."

That is a useful lesson. The operative values of the powerful are rarely articulated with such candor and precision. To be fair, they are not a U.S. monopoly. The values are shared by state/private power centers in other parliamentary democracies, and by their counterparts in societies where there is no need to indulge in rhetorical flourishes about "democracy."

The lessons are crystal clear. It would take real talent to miss them, and to fail to see how well they illustrate Madison's warnings over 200 years ago, when he deplored "the daring depravity of the times" as the "stockjobbers will become the pretorian band of the government—at once its tools and its tyrant; bribed by its largesses, and overawing it by clamors and combinations."

These observations reach to the core of the MAI. Like much of public policy in recent years, particularly in Anglo-American societies, the treaty is designed to undercut democracy and rights of citizens by transferring even more decision-making authority to unaccountable private institutions, the governments for whom they are "the domestic constituencies," and the international organizations with whom they share "common interests."

The Terms of the MAI

What do the terms of the MAI actually state, and portend? If the facts and issues were allowed to reach the public arena, what would we discover?

There can be no definite answer to such questions. Even if we had the full text of the MAI, a detailed list of the reservations introduced by signatories, and the entire verbatim record of the proceedings, we would not know the answers. The reason is that the answers are not determined by words, but by the power relations that impose their interpretations. Two centuries ago, in the leading democracy of his day, Oliver Goldsmith observed that "laws grind the poor, and rich men make the law"—the *operative* law, that is, whatever fine words may say. The principle remains valid.[17]

These are, again, truisms, with broad application. In the U.S. Constitution and its amendments, one can find nothing that authorizes the grant of human rights (speech, freedom from search and seizure, the right to buy elections, etc.) to what legal historians call "collectivist legal entities," organic entities that have the rights of "immortal persons"—rights far beyond those of real persons, when we take into account their power, and rights now being extended to those of states, as we have seen. One will search the UN Charter in vain to discover the basis for the authority claimed by Washington to use force and violence to achieve "the national interest," as defined by the immortal persons who cast over society the shadow called "politics," in John Dewey's evocative phrase. The U.S. Code defines "terrorism" with great clarity, and U.S. law provides severe penalties for the crime. But one will find no wording that exempts "the architects of power" from punishment for their exercises of state terror, not to speak of their monstrous clients (as long as they enjoy Washington's good graces): Suharto, Saddam Hussein, Mobutu, Noriega, and others great and small. As the leading human rights organizations point out year after year, virtually all U.S. foreign aid is illegal, from the leading recipient on down the list, because the law bars aid to countries that engage in "systematic torture." That may be law, but is it the meaning of the law?

The MAI falls into the same category. There is a "worst case" analysis, which will be the right analysis if "power remains in the dark," and the corporate lawyers who are its hired hands are able to establish their interpretation of the purposely convoluted and ambiguous wording of the draft treaty. There are less threatening interpretations, and they could turn out to be the right ones, if the "ultimate weapon" cannot be contained, and democratic procedures influence outcomes. Among these possible outcomes is the dismantling of the whole structure and the illegitimate institutions on which it rests. These are matters for popular organization and action, not words.

Here one might raise criticism of some of the critics of the MAI (myself included). The texts spell out the rights of "investors," not citizens, whose rights are correspondingly diminished. Critics accordingly call it an "investor rights agreement," which is true enough, but misleading. Just who are the "investors"?

Half the stocks in 1997 were owned by the wealthiest 1 percent of households, and almost 90 percent by the wealthiest tenth (concentration is still higher for bonds and trusts, comparable for other assets); adding pension plans leads only to slightly more even distribution among the top fifth of households. The enthusiasm about the radical asset inflation of recent years is understandable. And effective control of the corporation lies in very few institutional and personal hands, with the backing of law, after a century of judicial activism.[18]

Talk of "investors" should not conjure up pictures of Joe Doakes on the plant floor, but of the Caterpillar Corporation, which has just succeeded in breaking a major strike by reliance on the foreign investment that is so highly lauded: using the remarkable profit growth it shares with other "domestic constituencies" to create excess capacity abroad to undermine efforts by working people in Illinois to resist the erosion of their wages and working conditions. These developments result in no slight measure from the financial liberalization of the past twenty-five years, which is to be enhanced by the MAI; it is worth noting too that this era of financial liberalization has been one of unusually slow growth (including the current "boom," the poorest recovery in postwar history), low wages, high profits—and, incidentally, trade restrictions by the rich.

A better term for the MAI and similar endeavors is not "investor rights agreements" but "corporate rights agreements."

The relevant "investors" are collectivist legal entities, not persons as understood by common sense and the tradition, before the days when modern judicial activism created contemporary corporate power. That leads to another criticism. Opponents of the MAI often allege that the agreements grant too many rights to corporations. But to speak of granting too many rights to the king, or the dictator, or the slaveowner, is to give away too much ground. Rather than "corporate rights agreements," these measures might be termed, more accurately, "corporate power agreements," since it is hardly clear why such institutions should have any rights at all.

When the corporatization of the state capitalist societies took place a century ago, in part in reaction to massive market failures, conservatives—a breed that now scarcely exists—objected to this attack on the fundamental principles of classical liberalism. And rightly so. One may recall Adam Smith's critique of the "joint stock companies" of his day, particularly if management is granted a degree of independence; and his attitude toward the inherent corruption of private power, probably a "conspiracy against the public" when businessmen meet for lunch, in his acid view, let alone when they form collectivist legal entities and alliances among them, with extraordinary rights granted, backed, and enhanced by state power.

With these provisos in mind, let us recall some of the intended features of the MAI, relying on what information has reached the concerned public, thanks to the "unholy alliance."

"Investors" are accorded the right to move assets freely, including production facilities and financial assets, without "government interference" (meaning a voice for the public). By modes of chicanery familiar to the business world and corporate lawyers, the rights granted to foreign investors transfer easily to domestic investors as well. Among democratic choices that might be barred are those calling for local ownership, sharing of technology, local managers, corporate accountability, living wage provisions, preferences (for deprived areas, minorities, women, etc.), labor-consumer-environmental protection, restrictions on dangerous products, small business protection, support for strategic and emerging industries, land reform, community and worker control (that is, the foundations of authentic democracy), labor actions (which could be construed as illegal threats to order), and so on.

"Investors" are permitted to sue governments at any level for infringement on the rights granted them. There is no reciprocity: citizens and governments cannot sue "investors." The Ethyl and Metalclad suits are exploratory initiatives.

No restrictions are allowed on investment in countries with human rights violations: South Africa in the days of "constructive engagement," Burma today. It is to be understood, of course, that the Don will not be hampered by such constraints. The powerful stand above treaties and laws.

Constraints on capital flow are barred: for example, the conditions imposed by Chile to discourage inflows of short-term capital, widely credited with having insulated Chile somewhat from the destructive impact of highly volatile financial markets subject to unpredictable herdlike irrationality. Or more far-reaching measures that might well reverse the deleterious consequences of liberalizing capital flows. Serious proposals to achieve these ends have been on the table for years, but have never reached the agenda of the "architects of power." It may well be that the economy is harmed by financial liberalization, as the evidence suggests. But that is a matter of little moment in comparison with the advantages conferred by the liberalization of financial flows for a quarter century, initiated by the governments of the United States and U.K., primarily. These advantages are substantial. Financial liberalization contributes to concentration of wealth and provides powerful weapons to undermine social programs. It helps bring about the "significant wage restraint" and "atypical restraint on compensation increases [that] appears to be mainly the consequence of greater worker insecurity" that so encourage Fed chair Alan Greenspan and the Clinton Administration, sustaining the "economic miracle" that arouses awe among its beneficiaries and deluded observers, particularly abroad.

There are few surprises here. The designers of the post-World War II international economic system advocated freedom of trade but regulation of capital; that was the basic framework of the Bretton Woods system of 1944, including the charter of the IMF. One reason was the (rather plausible) expectation that liberalization of finance would impede freedom of trade. Another was the recognition that it would serve as a powerful weapon against democracy and the welfare state, which had enormous public support. Regulation of capital would allow governments to carry out monetary and tax policies and to sustain full employment and social programs without fear of capital flight, U.S. negotiator Harry Dexter White pointed out, with the agreement of his British counterpart, John Maynard Keynes. Free flow of capital, in contrast, would create what some international economists call a "virtual senate," in which highly concentrated financial capital imposes its own social policies on reluctant populations, punishing governments that deviate by capital flight.[19] The Bretton Woods assumptions largely prevailed during the "Golden Age" of high levels of growth of the economy and productivity, and extension of the social contract, through the 1950s and 1960s. The system was dismantled by Richard Nixon with the support of Britain, and, later, other major powers. The new orthodoxy became institutionalized as part of the "Washington consensus." Its outcomes conform rather well to the expectations of the designers of the Bretton Woods system.

Enthusiasm for the "economic miracles" wrought by the new orthodoxy is ebbing, however, among the managers of the global economy, as the near disasters that have accelerated since financial flows were liberalized from the 1970s have begun to threaten the "domestic constituencies" as well as the general public. Chief economist of the World Bank Joseph Stiglitz, the editors of the London *Financial Times*, and others close to the centers of power have begun to call for steps to regulate capital flows, following the lead of such bastions of respectability as the Bank for International Settlements. The World Bank has also somewhat reversed course. Not only is the global economy very poorly understood, but serious weaknesses are becoming harder to ignore and patch over. There may be changes, in unpredictable directions.[20]

Returning to the MAI, signatories are to be "locked in" for

twenty years. That is a "U.S. government proposal," according to the spokesperson for the Canadian Chamber of Commerce, who doubles as senior adviser of investment and trade for IBM Canada, and is selected to represent Canada in public debate.[21]

The treaty has a built-in "ratchet" effect, a consequence of provisions for "standstill" and "rollback." "Standstill" means that no new legislation is permitted that is interpreted as "nonconforming" to the MAI. "Rollback" means that governments are expected to eliminate legislation already on the books that is interpreted as "nonconforming." Interpretation, in all cases, is by you-know-who. The goal is to "lock countries in to" arrangements that, over time, will shrink the public arena more and more, transferring power to the approved "domestic constituencies" and their international structures. These include a rich array of corporate alliances to administer production and trade, relying on powerful states that are to maintain the system while socializing cost and risk for nationally based transnational corporations—virtually all TNCs, according to recent technical studies.

The target date for signing the MAI was April 27, 1998, but as it approached, it became clear that delays would be likely because of rising popular protest and disputes within the club. According to rumors filtering through the organs of power (mainly the foreign business press), these include efforts by the European Union and the United States to allow certain rights to constituent states, EU efforts to gain something like the vast internal market that U.S.-based corporations enjoy, reservations by France and Canada to maintain some control over their cultural industries (a far greater threat to smaller countries), and European objections to the more extreme and arrogant forms of U.S. market interference, such as the Helms-Burton act.

The *Economist* reports further problems. Labor and environmental issues, which "barely featured at the start," are becoming harder to suppress. It is becoming more difficult to ignore the paranoids and flat-earthers who "want high standards written in for how foreign investors treat workers and protect the environment," and "their fervent attacks, spread via a network of Internet web sites, have left negotiators unsure how to proceed." One possibility would be to pay attention to what the public wants. But that option is not mentioned: it is excluded in principle, since it would undermine the whole point of the enterprise.

Even if deadlines are not met and the effort is abandoned, that wouldn't show that it has "all been for nothing," the *Economist* informs its constituency. Progress has been made, and "with luck, parts of MAI could become a blueprint for a global WTO accord on investment," which the recalcitrant "developing countries" may be more willing to accept—after a few years of battering by market irrationalities, the subsequent discipline imposed on the victims by the world rulers, and growing awareness by elite elements that they can share in concentrated privilege by helping to disseminate the doctrines of the powerful, however fraudulent they may be, however others may fare. We can expect "parts of MAI" to take shape elsewhere, perhaps in the IMF, which is suitably secretive.

From another point of view, further delays have given the rascal multitude more opportunity to rend the veil of secrecy.

It is important for the general population to discover what is being planned for them. The efforts of governments and media to keep it all under wraps, except to their officially recognized "domestic constituencies," are surely understandable. But such barriers have been overcome by vigorous public action before, and can be again.

Originally published in Z, May 1998 as
"Domestic Constituencies."

Notes

1. See my articles in Z at the time; for review, Noam Chomsky, *World Orders, Old and New* (Columbia University Press, 1994), also Chapters IV

and V above. Glenn Burins, "Labor Fights Against Fast-Track Trade Measure," *Wall Street Journal*, September 16, 1997.

2. Bob Davis, *Wall Street Journal*, October 3, 1997.

3. Bruce Clark, "Pentagon Strategists Cultivate Defense Ties with Indonesia," *Financial Times*, March 23, 1998. 1965, see Noam Chomsky, *Year 501* (South End, 1993), Chapter 4. JFK/Colombia, see Michael McClintock, in Alexander George, ed., *Western State Terrorism* (Polity, 1991) and *Instruments of Statecraft* (Pantheon, 1992). Cuba: Nancy Dunne, *Financial Times*, March 24, 1998.

4. Jane Bussey, "New Rules Could Guide International Investment," *Miami Herald*, July 20, 1997.

5. Anthony Mason, "Are Our Sovereign Rights at Risk?" *The Age*, March 4, 1998.

6. *Economist*, March 21, 1998.

7. See note 9, below.

8. There are inconsistent claims about more recent availability. David Forman, *Australian*, January 14; Tim Colebatch, "Inquiry Call over 'Veil of Secrecy'" *Age*, March 4, 1998; editorials, *Australian*, March 9, 12; 1998 editorial, *Age*, March 14, 1998.

9. Laura Eggertson, "Treaty to Trim Ottawa's Power," *Toronto Globe and Mail*, April 3, 1997; *Macleans*, April 28, September 1, 1997; CBC, October 30, December 10, 1997. See *Monetary Reform* (Shanty Bay, Ontario), no. 7 (Winter 1997-1998). On the WTO, see Martin Khor, "Trade and Investment: Fighting over Investors' Rights at WTO," *Third World Economics* (Penang), February 15, 1997. Draft text: OECD, *Multilateral Agreement on Investment: Consolidated Texts and Commentary* (OLIS January 9, 1997; DAFFE/MAI/97; Confidential); available from Preamble Center for Public Policy (1737 21st St. NW, Washington, D.C. 20009). Drafts with later dates have also been cited; e.g., Martin Khor, *Third World Economics*, February 1-15, 1998, citing OECD, October 1, 1997. See Scott Nova and Michelle Sforza-Roderick of Preamble, "M.I.A. Culpa," *Nation*, January 13, 1997; also other reports in the independent ("alternative") press. For more information, see Maude Barlow and Tony Clarke, *MAI and the Threat to American Freedom* (New York: Stoddart, 1998); International Forum on Globalization (1555 Pacific Avenue, San Francisco, CA 94109); Public Citizen's Global Trade Watch (215 Pennsylvania Avenue SE, Washington, D.C. 20003); Preamble Center; People's Global Action (playfair@asta.rwth-aachen.de).

10. Samuel Huntington, *American Politics: The Promise of Disharmony* (Harvard University Press, 1981); cited by Sidney Plotkin and William Scheurmann, *Private Interests, Public Spending* (South End, 1994), 223. Huntington, "Vietnam Reappraised," *International Security*, Summer 1981.

11. House letter on MAI, to President Clinton; November 5, 1997.

12. Laura Eggertson, "Ethyl Sues Ottawa over MMT Law," *G&M*, April 15, 1997; *Third World Economics*, June 30, 1997; *Briefing Paper: Ethyl Corporation v. Government of Canada*, Preamble Center for Public Policy, n.d.; Joel Millman, *Wall Street Journal*, October 14, 1997. Technically, the new law only bans importation and interprovincial trade of MMT, but that is effectively a ban, since only Ethyl produces or sells MMT. Canada later capitulated and lifted the ban, unwilling to face a costly suit. John Urquhart, *Wall Street Journal*, July 21, 1998. Canada is now facing new charges of "expropriation" from the U.S. hazardous waste disposal company S.D. Myers, again under NAFTA rules, referring to a Canadian ban on export of highly toxic PCBs. Scott Morrison and Edward Alden, *Financial Times*, September 2, 1998.

13. A current example is the suit brought by the nursing home chain Beverly Enterprises against Cornell University labor historian Kate Bronfenbrenner, who testified on its practices at a town meeting, at the invitation of members of the Pennsylvania congressional delegation (personal communication; also Steven Greenhouse, *NYT*, April 1, 1998; Deidre McFadyen, *In These Times*, April 5, 1998). For Beverly, the outcome is largely irrelevant, since discovery demands alone severely damage Professor Bronfenbrenner and her university, and may have a chilling effect on other researchers and educational institutions.

14. White House letter, January 20, 1998. I am indebted to congressional staffers, particularly the office of Representative Bernie Sanders.

15. Jane Bussey, "New Rules Could Guide International Investment," *Miami Herald*, July 20, 1997; R.C. Longworth, "New Rules for Global Economy," *Chicago Tribune*, December 4, 1997. See also Jim Simon, *Seattle Times*, "Environmentalists Suspicious of Foreign-Investor-Rights Plan," *Seattle Times*, November 22, 1997; Lorraine Woellert, "Trade Storm Brews over Corporate Rights," *Washington Times*, December 15, 1997. *Business Week*, February 9, 1998; *NYT*, February 13, 1998, paid advertisement; NPR, *Morning Edition*, February 16, 1998; Peter Ford, *Christian Science Monitor*, February 28, 1998; Peter Beinart, *New Republic*, December 15, 1997; Fred Hiatt, *Washington Post*, April 1, 1998.

16. "The Multilateral Agreement on Investment," statement by Undersecretary of State Stuart Eizenstat and Deputy U.S. Trade Representative Jeffrey Lang, February 17, 1998.

17. Oliver Goldsmith, "The Traveller" (1765).

18. Lawrence Mishel, Jared Bernstein, and John Schmitt, *The State of Working America; 1996-97* (Economic Policy Institute: M.E. Sharpe, 1997). On the legal background, see particularly Morton Horwitz, *The Transformation of American Law, 1870-1960* (Oxford University Press, 1992), Chapter 3.

19. Eric Helleiner, *States and Reemergence of Global Finance* (Cornell, 1994); James Mahon, *Mobile Capital and Latin American Development* (Pennsylvania State University, 1996).

20. Helleiner, *op. cit.*, 190; editorial, "Regulating Capital Flows," *Financial Times*, March 25, 1998; Joseph Stiglitz, same day; *The State in a Changing World: World Development Report 1997* (World Bank, 1997). These developments have been regularly reviewed in highly insightful analyses by international economist David Felix, most recently in his "Asia and the Crisis of Financial Liberalization," in Dean Baker, Gerald Epstein, and Robert Pollin, eds., *Globalization and Progressive Economic Policy* (Cambridge University Press, 1998).

21. Doug Gregory, St. Lawrence Center Forum, November 18, 1997; reprinted in *Monetary Reform, no. 7* (Winter 1997-98).

22. See Guy de Jonquières, "Axe over Hopes for MAI Accord," *Financial Times*, March 25, 1998; *Economist*, March 21, 1998.

VII

"Hordes
of
Vigilantes"

Chapter VI went to press a few weeks before the April 1998 target date for signing of the MAI by the OECD countries. At the time, it was fairly clear that agreement would not be reached, and it was not—an important event, worth considering carefully as a lesson in what can be achieved by the "ultimate weapon" of popular organizing and activism, even under highly inauspicious circumstances.

In part, the failure resulted from internal disputes—for example, European objections to the U.S. federal system and the extraterritorial reach of U.S. laws, concerns about maintaining some degree of cultural autonomy, and so on. But a much more significant problem was looming: massive public opposition world-wide. It was becoming increasingly difficult to ensure that the rules of global order would continue to be "written by the lawyers and businessmen who plan to benefit" and "by governments taking advice and guidance from these lawyers and businessmen," while "invariably, the thing missing is the public voice"—the *Chicago Tribune*'s accurate description of the negotiations for the MAI, as well as ongoing efforts to "craft rules" for "global activity" in other domains without public interference. It was, in short, becoming more difficult to restrict awareness and engagement to sectors identified by the Clinton Administration, with unusual and unintended clarity, as its "domestic constituencies": the U.S. Council for International Business, which "advances the global interests of American business both at home and abroad," and concentrations of private power generally—but crucially not Congress (which had not been informed, in violation of constitutional requirements) and the general public, its voice stilled by a "veil of secrecy" that was maintained with impressive discipline during three years of intensive negotiations.[1]

The problem had been pointed out by the London *Economist* as the target date approached. Information was leaking through public interest groups and grassroots organizations, and it was becoming harder to ignore those who "want high standards written in for how foreign investors treat workers and protect the environment," issues that "barely featured" as long as deliberations were restricted to the "domestic constituencies" of the democratic states.[2]

As expected, the OECD countries did not reach agreement on April 27, 1998, and we move to the next phase. One useful consequence was that the national press departed from its (virtual) silence. In the business pages of the *New York Times*, economic affairs correspondent Louis Uchitelle reported that the target date for the MAI had been delayed six months, under popular pressure. Treaties concerning trade and investment usually "draw little public attention" (why?); and while "labor and the environment are not excluded," the director of international trade at the National Association of Manufacturers explained, "they are not at the center" of the concerns of trade diplomats and the World Trade Organization. But "these outsiders are clamoring to make their views known in the negotiations for a treaty that is to be called the Multilateral Agreement on Investment," Uchitelle commented (with intended irony, I presume), and the clamor sufficed to compel the delay.

The Clinton Administration, "acknowledging the pressure," strove to present the matter in the proper light. Its representative at the MAI negotiations said, "There is strong support for measures in the treaty that would advance this country's environmental goals and our agenda on international labor standards." So the clamoring outsiders are pushing an open door: Washington has been the most passionate advocate of their cause, they should be relieved to discover.

The *Washington Post* also reported the delay, in its financial section, blaming primarily "the French intelligentsia," who had "seized on the idea" that the rules of the MAI "posed a threat to French culture," joined by Canadians as well. "And the Clinton Administration showed little interest in fighting for the accord, especially given fervent opposition from many of the same American environmental and labor groups that battled against [NAFTA]," and that somehow fail to comprehend that their battle is misdirected, since it is the Clinton Administration that has been insisting upon "environmental goals" and "international labor standards" all along—not an outright falsehood, since the goals and standards are left suitably vague.[3]

That labor "battled against NAFTA" is the characteristic way of presenting the fact that the labor movement called for a version of NAFTA that would serve the interests of the people of the three countries involved, not just investors; and that their detailed critique and proposals were barred from the media (as were the similar analyses and proposals of Congress's Office of Technology Assessment).

Time reported that the deadline was missed "in no small part because of the kind of activism on display in San Jose," California, referring to a demonstration by environmentalists and others. "The charge that the MAI would eviscerate national environmental protections has turned a technical economic agreement into a *cause célèbre*." The observation was amplified in the Canadian press, which alone in the Western world began to cover the topic seriously (under intense pressure by popular organizations and activists) after only two years of silence. The *Toronto Globe and Mail* observed that the OECD governments "were no match...for a global band of grassroots organizations, which, with little more than computers and access to the Internet, helped derail a deal."[4]

The same theme was voiced with a note of despair, if not terror, by the world's leading business daily, the *Financial Times* of London. In an article headlined "Network Guerrillas," it reported that "fear and bewilderment have seized governments of industrialised countries" as, "to their consternation," their efforts to impose the MAI in secret "have been ambushed by a horde of vigilantes whose motives and methods are only dimly understood in most national capitals"—naturally enough; they are not among the "domestic constituencies," so how can governments be expected to understand them? "This week the horde claimed its first success" by blocking the agreement on the MAI, the journal continued, "and some think it could fundamentally alter the way international economic agreements are negotiated."

The hordes are a terrifying sight: "they included trade unions, environmental and human rights lobbyists, and pressure groups opposed to globalisation"—meaning, globalization in the particular form demanded by the "domestic constituencies." The rampaging horde overwhelmed the pathetic and helpless power structures of the rich industrial societies. They are led by "fringe movements that espouse extreme positions" and have "good organisation and strong finances" that enable them "to wield much influence with the media and members of national parliaments." In the United States, the "much influence" with the media was effectively zero, and in Britain, which hardly differed, it reached such heights that Home Secretary Jack Straw of the Labor government conceded over BBC that he had never heard of the MAI. But it must be understood that even the slightest breach in conformity is a terrible danger.

The journal goes on to urge that it will be necessary "to drum up business support" so as to beat back the hordes. Until now, business hasn't recognized the severity of the threat. And it is severe indeed. "Veteran trade diplomats" warn that with "growing demands for greater openness and accountability," it is becoming "harder for negotiators to do deals behind closed doors and submit them for rubber-stamping by parliaments." "Instead, they face pressure to gain wider popular legitimacy for their actions by explaining and defending them in public," no easy task when the hordes are concerned about "social and economic security," and when the impact of trade agreements "on ordinary people's lives…risks stirring up popular resentment" and "sensitivities over issues such as environmental and food safety standards." It might even become impossible "to resist demands for direct participation by lobby groups in WTO decisions, which would violate one of the body's central principles": "'This is the place where governments collude in private against their domestic pressure groups,' says a former WTO official." If the walls are breached, the WTO and similar secret organizations of the rich and powerful might be turned into "a happy hunting ground for special interests": workers, farmers, people concerned about social and economic security and food safety and the fate of future generations, and other extremist fringe elements who do not understand that resources are efficiently used when they are directed to short-term profit for private power, served by the governments that "collude in private" to protect and enhance their power.[5]

It is superfluous to add that the lobbies and pressure groups that are causing such fear and consternation are not the U.S. Council for International Business, the "lawyers and businessmen" who are "writing the rules of global order," and the like, but the "public voice" that is "invariably missing."

The "collusion in private" goes well beyond trade agreements, of course. The responsibility of the public to assume cost and risk is, or should be, well known to observers of what its acolytes like to call the "free enterprise capitalist economy." In the same article, Uchitelle reports that Caterpillar, which recently relied on excess production capacity abroad to break a major strike, has moved 25 percent of its production abroad and aims to increase sales from abroad by 50 percent by 2010, with the assistance of U.S. taxpayers: "The Export-Import Bank plays a significant role in [Caterpillar's] strategy," with "low-interest credits" to facilitate the operation. Ex-Im credits already provide close to 2 percent of Caterpillar's $19 billion annual revenue and will rise with new projects planned in China. That is standard operating procedure: multinational corporations typically rely on the home state for crucial services.[6] "In really tough, high-risk, high-opportunity markets," a Caterpillar executive explains, "you really have to have someone in your corner," and governments—especially powerful ones—"will always have greater leverage" than banks and greater willingness to offer low-interest loans, thanks to the largesse of the unwitting taxpayer.

Management is to remain in the U.S., so the people who count will be close to the protector in their corner and will enjoy a proper lifestyle, with the landscape improved as well: the hovels of the foreign work force will not mar the view. Profits aside, the operation provides a useful weapon against workers who dare to raise their heads (as the recent strike illustrates), and who help out by paying for the loss of their jobs and for the improved weapons of class war. What's more, all of this improves the health of the "fairy tale economy," which relies on "greater worker insecurity," as the experts explain.

In the conflict over the MAI, the lines could not have been more starkly drawn. On one side are the industrial democracies and their "domestic constituencies." On the other, the "hordes of vigilantes," "special interests," and "fringe extremists" who call for openness and accountability and are displeased when parliaments simply rubber-stamp the secret deals of the state-private power nexus. The hordes were confronting the major concentration of power in the world, arguably in world history: the governments of the rich and powerful states, the international financial institutions, and the concentrated financial and manufacturing sectors, including the corporate media. And popular elements won—despite resources so minuscule and organization so limited that only the paranoia of those who demand absolute power could perceive the outcome in the terms just reviewed. That is a remarkable achievement.

It's not the only such victory in the same few months. Another was achieved in the fall of 1997, when the administration was compelled to withdraw its proposed "Fast Track" legislation. Recall that the issue was not "free trade," as commonly alleged, but democracy: the demand of the hordes "for greater openness and accountability." The Clinton Administration had argued, correctly, that it was asking for nothing new: just the same authority its predecessors had enjoyed to conduct "deals behind closed doors" that are submitted "for rubber-stamping by parliaments." But times are changing. As the business press recognized when "Fast Track" faced an unexpected public challenge, opponents of the old regime had an "ultimate weapon," the general population, which was no longer satisfied to keep to the spectator role as their betters did the important work. The complaints of the business press echo those of the liberal internationalists of the Trilateral Commission twenty-five years ago, lamenting the efforts of the "special interests" to organize and enter the political arena. Their vulgar antics disrupted the civilized arrangements that had prevailed before the "crisis of democracy" erupted, when "Truman had been able to govern the country with the cooperation of a relatively small number of Wall Street lawyers and bankers," as explained by Harvard's Samuel Huntington, soon to become professor of the Science of Government. And now they are intruding in even more sacred chambers.

These are important developments. The OECD powers and their domestic constituencies are of course not going to accept defeat. They will undertake more efficient public relations to explain to the hordes that they are better off keeping to their private pursuits while the business of the world is conducted in secret, and they will seek ways to implement the MAI in the OECD or some other framework.[7] Efforts are already underway to change the IMF charter to impose MAI-style provisions as conditions on credits, thus enforcing the rules for the weak, ultimately others. The really powerful will follow their own rules, as when the Clinton Administration interrupted its passionate pleas for free trade to slap prohibitive tariffs on Japanese supercomputers that were undercutting U.S. manufacturers (called "private," despite their massive dependency on public subsidy and protection).[8]

Though power and privilege surely will not rest, nonetheless the popular victories should be heartening. They teach lessons about what can be achieved even when opposing forces are so outlandishly unbalanced as in the MAI confrontation. It is true that such victories are defensive. They prevent, or at least delay, steps to undermine democracy even further, and to transfer even more power into the hands of the rapidly concentrating private tyrannies that seek to administer markets and to constitute a "virtual Senate" that has many ways to block popular efforts to use democratic forms for the public interest: threat of capital flight, transfer of production, media control, and other means. One should attend carefully to the fear and desperation of the powerful. They understand very well the potential reach of the "ultimate weapon," and only hope that those who seek a more free and just world will not gain the same understanding, and put it effectively to use.

This article was originally published in Z, July/August 1998.

Notes

1. R. C. Longworth, "Global Markets Become a Private Business: Experts Begin Setting the Rules Away from Public View," *Chicago Tribune-Denver Post*, May 7, 1998.

2. *Economist*, March 21, 1998.

3. Louis Uchitelle, *NYT*, April 30, 1998; Anna Swardson, *Washington Post*, datelined April 29, 1998.

4. *Time*, April 27, 1998, *G&M*, April 29, 1998; both cited in *Weekly News Update*, Nicaragua Solidarity Network, 339 Lafayette St., New York, NY 10012.

5. Guy de Jonquières, "Network Guerrillas", *Financial Times* (London), April 30, 1998. Jack Straw cited in David Smith, "The Whole World in Their Hands," *Sunday Times* (London), May 17, 1998. A database search of the British media by Simon Finch found virtually no articles on the MAI before 1998.

6. For extensive evidence, see Winfried Ruigrock and Rob van Tulder, *The Logic of International Restructuring* (Routledge, 1995).

7. Regular updates are available from Public Citizen's Global Trade Watch, 215 Pennsylvania Ave SE, Washington, D.C. 20003; http://www.citizen.org/pctrade/tradehome.html.

8. Bob Davis, "In Effect, ITC's Steep Tariffs on Japan Protect U.S. Makers of Supercomputers," *Wall Street Journal,* September 29, 1997.

NOAM CHOMSKY was born on December 7, 1928 in Philadelphia, Pennsylvania. His undergraduate and graduate years were spent at the University of Pennsylvania where he received his Ph.D. in linguistics in 1955. During the years 1951 to 1955, Chomsky was a Junior Fellow of the Harvard University Society of Fellows. While a Junior Fellow he completed his doctoral dissertation entitled, "Transformational Analysis." The major theoretical viewpoints of the dissertation appeared in the monograph *Syntactic Structure*, which was published in 1957. This formed part of a more extensive work, *The Logical Structure of Linguistic Theory*, circulated in mimeograph in 1955 and published in 1975.

Chomsky joined the staff of the Massachusetts Institute of Technology in 1955 and in 1961 was appointed full professor in the Department of Modern Languages and Linguistics (now the Department of Linguistics and Philosophy). From 1966 to 1976 he held the Ferrari P. Ward Professorship of Modern Languages and Linguistics. In 1976 he was appointed Institute Professor.

During the years 1958 to 1959 Chomsky was in residence at the Institute for Advanced Study at Princeton, NJ. In the spring of 1969 he delivered the John Locke Lectures at Oxford; in January 1970 he delivered the Bertrand Russell Memorial Lecture in New Delhi, and in 1977, the Huizinga Lecture in Leiden, among many others.

Professor Chomsky has received honorary degrees from the University of London, the University of Chicago, Swarthmore College, Delhi University, Bard College, the University of Massachusetts, the University of Pennsylvania, Amherst College, Cambridge University, and the University of Buenos Aires. He is a Fellow of the American Academy of Arts and Sciences and the National Academy of Science. In addition, he is a member of other professional and learned societies in the United States and abroad, and is a recipient of the Distinguished Scientific Contribution Award of the American Psychological Association, the Kyoto Prize in Basic Sciences, the Helmholtz Medal, and others.

Chomsky has written and lectured widely on linguistics, philosophy, intellectual history, contemporary issues, international affairs and U.S. foreign policy.

ROBERT W. McCHESNEY is Associate Professor of Communication at the University of Illinois at Urbana-Champaign. He is the author of several books, including *Telecommunications, Mass Media, and Democracy* (Oxford University Press, 1993), *Corporate Media and the Threat to Democracy* (Seven Stories, 1997), and the forthcoming *Rich Media, Poor Democracy: Communication Politics in Dubious Times* (University of Illinois Press, 1999).